LET THE
DECl

A CHELSEA TALE FROM BARCELONA AND MUNICH

WALTER OTTON

LET THE CELERY DECIDE
A Chelsea tale from Barcelona and Munich

Twitter: @WalterOtton
cover photograph: Walter Otton
cover design: Tom Morton
www.gate17.co.uk

CONTENTS

Part One

Part Two

NISI DOMINUS FRUSTRA
Without God all is in vain.
Chelsea coat of arms, 1903, inspired by Psalm 127

"Rain fell first light, but it got heavier. Water smashed the ground like bullets against the floor. Puddles grew bigger and bigger connecting with each other, making one puddle covering the whole town. A damp, misty fog hung over the area obscuring people's view. The water disappeared because the sun came out."

Sol Benjamin, aged 11 (eleven).

DEDICATION
To my friends Andrew S, Christopher S, Jonathan T, Paul B.

PART ONE

"In the most testing circumstances.... (ref blows the full-time whistle) – THEY'VE DONE IT! It's a night Chelsea will NEVER forget. One of the greatest moments in their history – they have triumphed here against the odds."

Alan Parry, commentator, Camp Nou, Tuesday 24th April 2012

Chapter One

GATWICK

Monday 23rd April 2012

I open my eyes at around half-five am, my arms hugging my body and my back hunched against the airport wall. I begin trying to focus on the screen across the floor – it's only a small distance away – I could step closer to it, but this is where I told Larry I'd meet him, plus I need the wall to support me to stand upright. I look to the ceiling and study it before tightly closing my eyes shut once more hoping the shadows don't reappear – I open my eyes and blink – everything is a little snowy. I blink again, then return my gaze to the monitor, squinting at the display that lists all the upcoming destinations. I'm trying to make out the City of Valencia displayed in orange lights on the screen, but when the snow noticeably thickens and falls heavier in front of my eyes, I close them in surrender, letting the snow fall behind my eyelids instead. Open or closed, the flakes fall, but I'd rather the flakes than the shadows.

I know a wave of nausea is imminent. I brace myself; anticipating it to come rolling in on the wind of the snowy clouds. In preparation, I crouch down, putting my head between my legs, purposefully breathing slowly and hoping the waves do not submerge me. Squatting, I hear the Doctor's words: *You've got all the signs of a breakdown* then something about *nervous exhaustion and clinical depression* followed by *it'll take at least a year to recover* and now I'm in that limbo moment where either the nausea and panic and anxiety will start to batter me like rough sea over a beach groyne or it will subside – simply taunting my toes with an unwelcome sharp ripple. I imagine my father, it's the late seventies, and he's smacking his huge palm against the side of the Radio Rentals television set because the reception is on the blink. I gratefully sense the giddiness retreating – the nauseous gale has blown itself away and the snow flurries lighten bit by bit until they're gone – I take another breath, I fill my lungs with regurgitated air, hating the fact I'm trapped with thousands of other humans in an airport. Holding the air in, I stand upright. Exhaling, I open my eyes and see Larry walking towards me and I say to myself – *hello, sunshine* – expectant that his presence and friendship will be the light that crushes the darkness – but it's not like that – *something is wrong* – a haunting look hangs off his face, something I can't place – I've got our match tickets in my front right pocket, maybe he's lost his passport – no, it's something else – my gut turns a somersault – I can see that the skin under Larry's eyes is heavy and dark – his grey etched wrinkles make me think of a walrus – he smiles weakly and I think of the wide, scared eyes of a hungry child – I see a lost dog panicking for its owner or maybe that should be an owner panicking for their lost dog – either way, Larry looks like someone has died – and then I put two-and-two together – in a sense someone *has* died, even though they haven't actually been born yet – he and Liz must have found out on Friday and he's spent the weekend dealing with the fallout – three strikes and you're out – that's the deal with IVF treatment – they haven't got through their last effort of IVF – it's all over his face – grief for a child that will never be conceived – and I feel useless and guilty, like I've betrayed him because I have two children, and one of them wasn't planned – and he's done all the planning in the world and spent all the money in his bank and the weight on his shoulders is something I cannot lift from him, all I can do is be here, and here I am, and he is here with me.

I stand in the queue for the check-in, but I don't really feel I'm here – I'm swimming underwater with my eyes open but it's murky and I can't see where I'm swimming and I don't know how deep this River is – I've been off work for three months and the Doctor says it could be another nine months until I'm fit for work – as I dive deeper into the dark water I reflect that nine months is the term of a pregnancy – and maybe if I reach the bottom of this River I'll feel with my hands down on its bed and clasp a magic, golden lamp, and when I pull it out I'll clutch it towards my body and hold the lamp there securely until I break the water on the surface – I lift the magic, golden lamp up to Larry who has one wish and that wish is for Liz to conceive and for a child to be born unto them – they are one, joined in holy matrimony, they each vowed to the other to be there until death us do part – I can see their wedding invitation addressed to me, it was designed with a small rope attached to the envelope, three cords entwined. Larry is one cord, Liz the other, the third the love of God – three is stronger than two – there is no magic gold lamp though – just a passport

I'm handing over a bland counter to a lady with too much make-up on, the excessive blusher like an over-iced cake – I hear myself telling her that I packed my own bag while simultaneously I'm inwardly reflecting that maybe Larry should be with his wife, not with me going to watch Chelsea, but maybe Liz needs some space anyway to reflect and process and sing her heart out – boy, can she sing – that such a sound could come out of one so petite is a wonder – and I'm told that this was the way of Father Abraham's Sarah. Remember what Isaiah wrote: *Rejoice, barren woman who bears no children, shout and cry out, woman who has no birth pangs. Once you had no children, but now you will have more children than a woman who has been married for a long time.*

On the aeroplane I clip in my seat-belt and find myself staring at the metal clasp. I think of a zippo lighter flicking into life, the flame lifted to a cigarette end, the sound of burning tobacco, the chime of the zippo lid clacking shut, the taste that accompanies inhalation, chemicals coursing through the system – the craving is real, but it's a long time until I've fully exited Valencia airport before I smoke. Looking to my right, I study Larry who is in the window seat. He's leaning forward with his forehead resting against the back of the head rest in front of him. I can't discern the names of the weights that sit heavy on his shoulders, but I can see their shapes pushing down on his large frame, they are negatively changing and affecting the whole form of his posture, his back is bent, his knees straining under the pressure, his forehead light with mild sweat. As the aeroplane starts taxiing, the Captain's smooth tone comes over the speaker to gently announce the Cabin Crew's impending safety performance, Larry doesn't flinch, he's wholly focused on controlling his breathing, it's like no-one else is there.

I look up briefly at another female face with make-up covering a forced, fixed smile giving me and my fellow passengers instructions in her neat uniform about inflating my life-jacket by blowing into a little tube. I glance away because the shadows have returned in front of my eyes – but I don't go into a panic, instead I let them consume me – I picture the plane engine erupting in flame mid-flight and I find myself not caring and this invites laughter, a sound from deep in my gut – I'm laughing because if we crash and I sink, I don't even care – ha, for the first time in my life I don't give a fuck if this machine goes down. I'm on a plane but I'm in the valley of the shadow of death and I say *go on then, yeah, I'm ready to die* and I settle in my seat to get my back comfortable to be in a position to embrace the plane crash should it come – I look back at the stewardess acting out her duties – a Spanish young lady, a few years younger than me. I study her face, careful for it not to look like I'm staring, you know – I ascertain that her make-up has not been slapped on as excessively as the woman back at the airport behind the check-in desk. No, she hasn't rushed this morning – she has got up in plenty of time, tied her hair in a neat bun, mousey-brown roots but blonde dye doing its job – I wonder what it must feel like to be her – or anyone who works on aeroplanes – imagine having this mindset that you're not scared of flying – why would you be as Cabin Crew? It's truly a gift – I find myself wanting to explain to her that if the plane crashes, that, for the first time in my life, I don't care about plummeting down. I truly believe that my kids will be okay – I told my wife that I knew how life would pan out for her if my illness beat me – she would meet someone who would take care of her financially and take care of her emotionally and make all her dreams come true but – most of all, this new man in her life would not be traumatised by depression – he would not be crushed by darkness, he would not put his head under the parapet, he would not bottle out on life – he would be everything she needs and more – I mean, it's not like I've got cancer or anything – I'm a weakling, I know it and I embrace it – it is me – I cannot shake it off, I cannot snap out of it – yet through her tears, Josie told me not to talk like that, and I said *look I might not get better,* and she said *don't talk like that,* and I said *I trust that God would look after our kids* and she said *don't talk like that* and then the Doctor prescribed me something else for this clinical depression and I spent three days in bed hallucinating all kinds of darkness – that's when the shadows started circling and the falling snow followed – and maybe I'm still hallucinating now – those dark shapes on Larry's shoulders and that, and that's maybe why I suddenly don't give a fuck about flying today because depression is what it is, yes it is what it is – and I've surrendered to it – and like they say, every dog has it's day and like they say, every cloud has a silver lining – I find myself smiling for the first time ever during a take-off – the nose of the plane angles up as the engines roar into the South English sky and I think: *Though I walk through the valley of the shadow of death I will fear no evil, for You are with me.*

I put my head back and close my eyes, I feel tired, I feel old, I feel I need refreshing, I feel exhausted of feeling the need to describe what I've been prescribed. Chelsea the perfect antidote to the poison in my system. I search my memories purposefully, thoroughly – electrons pushing through the medicine in my brain to locate a memory to fit the occasion – I can't rush it, just relax into it, I've learnt to accept that if the memory disappears, it's okay, it means the time isn't right – but it is forming, it's not quite on the tip of my tongue, but I'm edging towards it; flicking through a rolodex, specially shaped index cards in alphabetical order – shuffling to the edge of a cliff – *THERE IT IS!* I pause at the rolodex at D. D is for Dancing Ledge – ha! Yes, Dancing Ledge in Swanage. It's Paulo's birthday, we've been camping nearby. George is primed to explain to us later how Dancing Ledge is part of the Jurassic Coast – giving us a brief outline of its history. We've scrambled down some rock, not much, maybe ten foot, and there is a perfect pool before us – the sea crashes in, tops up the pool, and then ripples away. Blue sky and blue water like a brochure. I ease my rucksack off my shoulders, pull my T-shirt off over my head, unlace my hiking boots, boots off, remove my shorts, toss aside my socks, take my old trainers from my rucksack, hurrying now, lace my old trainers up, stand alongside Paulo and George – together we count down: *Three! Two! One!* and we dive-bomb into the ocean – the sharp hit of cold sea water envelopes me, Dancing Ledge – what a beautiful name – I spend some seconds submerged, old soles of worn trainers keeping my old soles of worn skin from being nicked on rocks. Underwater, I circle my arms and upturned palms around to keep my crouched body on the rock bed – synchronised – I stay on the rock getting refreshed – I feel clean – a baptisms of sorts – I let the healing water do its job until my lungs start protesting and my ears pulsating, so I push up and break the surface to be welcomed by fresh air and blue sky and the laughter of friendship and I am more restored than I was yesterday, and I know this buzz, the very essence of this memory at Dancing Ledge, will be replicated – it will be mirrored in Valencia – I know it in my bones.

Stretching my legs out as much as space permits under the seat in front of me, I consider that as this aeroplane hurtles towards the east coast of the Iberian Peninsula that fronts the Gulf of Valencia on the Mediterranean Sea, I am transporting myself back to the day at Dancing Ledge, treading water in the pool under a perfect summer sky and hearing George explaining to all of us:

You see, the limestone was laid down 150-million-years ago – the limestone, you can see how it's all blocked. It's laid down horizontally as a sediment, lots of old fossils, layer upon layer – it's very resistant. It only erodes a few millimetres a year because it's blocked. The rainwater gets in-between and dissolves it – a bit of weather and carbonation and the blocks can fall off in one go. Now, if you look around at the floor, it's a perfect specimen of a wave-cut platform! So, the sea comes in over the rocks, but by the time it reaches here to Dancing Ledge, it has lost a lot of its energy. If you look here to the long crevice, this is the route of the old cliffs! So, all-in-all, what we are looking at here is an ultimate example of a wave-cut platform. Now, look to where I'm pointing – can you see that cave I'm pointing at? Yeah? Can you see those angular shapes? Some of that actually isn't natural – it's the result of humans quarrying. In the 1800s we removed loads of limestone to build places like Westminster Abbey and St. Paul's cathedral – sometimes I think about that – that from here in Swanage, the heart of the Jurassic Coastline, I can scramble down this section of cliff and swim at Dancing Ledge and the limestone was quarried to build such historic buildings. Mad, isn't it?

And then George punches the sky and dive-bombs in again. I swim towards the ledge, haul myself up and look out to the horizon for a few seconds before turning one-hundred-and-eighty degrees to launch myself in once more – as I jump, I can see Paulo out the corner of my eye in mid-air doing the same thing, too.

Chapter Two

VALENCIA

Monday 23rd April 2012

He's wearing a black polo T-shirt with black jeans and cherry red DMs – his jeans have a hole in the left knee – white string spread across his skin giving the impression that his knee is behind denim bars – his arms look strong, but the body under the black material is skinny. The geezer is some sort of poet, I reckon, maybe a musician – it's in his dark brown eyes – wide, taking in everything around him. I remember reading about musicians and wide eyes – the need to be needed – give me some love, give me some attention, like me for what I do – identical to the girl at the party craving some attention – the eyes don't dart around, they sweep gently across the room, panoramic – taking it all in, wanting a Prince Charming to bring her a drink and listen to her woes – walk her home – splash her some cigarettes – she pecks you on your cheek before she leaves you hanging right after you've put your hand on her waist – she ducks and swerves – the peck on your cheek was hollow, leaves you more vacant, you watch her close her front door behind her, shutting you out, you wish you had one more can of beer for your walk home but you dig your hands in your pockets instead – you've gone right out of your way walking her back from the party – boys will be boys and she's proper played you – but this geezer in his black attire and cherry red DMs ain't a teenage girl craving attention – but his eyes remind me of that, and I don't know why – he doesn't even know I'm intermittently glancing at him – and then my phone starts flashing on the table – it's on silent – but it's flashing – my Mum is ringing.

My first reaction is to push my phone away so I don't say the wrong thing, then I instantly feel regret and tell myself the sensible thing is to answer it. Mum talks about what to give my kids for dinner. I know that she knows what to give them for dinner; it's an excuse because she just wants to talk – I let her talk about the sausages she's got from the butchers and the potato mashed with soya milk as if I was worried my dairy intolerant children would be subjected to full-fat milk – and then I give my Mum space and she fills the silence by asking what she really wants to ask, which is: *am I all right?* And I tell her: *I'm fine, I'm away with Larry, remember?* Then she says she wondered why the ring-tone was all funny when she called me – and I said *that's how it sounds when you ring a number abroad* – and she apologises again and I tell her to stop saying sorry, it's all fine, she asks how Larry is and I tell her, *he's okay, this is the best place for him to be,* I don't tell her that half-an-hour ago he went for a walk and he hasn't come back, but I'm happy in my surroundings, I'm cool with letting her talk about her day shopping in the village for sausages and as she speaks, my glance focuses on a boy.

He is no more than four-years-old, he has his hand down the front of his T-shirt and placed it over his heart, he's proper stretching the fabric at the neck, his eyes grow wide with wonder as he exclaims: *Mama! Mama!* With his hand he pats his chest over his heart – it stretches his T-shirt some more, his Mama laughs and talks to him in quick-fire Spanish that I don't understand, I would love to know what she is saying to him, her son who has just discovered his heartbeat, maybe at his nursery they have been learning about looking at parts of the body, and this kid is over the moon that he can feel his heart thumping and his Mama is still smiling at the enthusiasm he is showing with his discovery. He starts to climb on her, puts his hands on his Mama's thighs, scrunches her lemon yellow dress with his fingers, a brown belt pulling the material tight around her waist, she pulls him up on to her lap and he puts his hand on her chest, but he's put it on the wrong side, so she gently takes his hand and moves it to the other side of her chest over her heart. His face holds still with concentration and curiosity, like a cat on a wall stepping towards a stranger who is walking past. I take my daze away from this intimate moment and look into my glass at my drink and focus my ears back into the voice of my own Mum on the phone telling me that Dad will be taking the car to the garage later, *hopefully it won't be too expensive,* and I miss the reaction of the son feeling his Mama's heartbeat on the palm of his hand. I cradle the phone between my ear and my shoulder and pull a cigarette out from my packet. My Mum hears my orange Clipper flick and spark followed by the sound of my inhalation, so she tuts and says my name gently and I say, *I know,* and she replies *think of your arteries* as I watch the smoke drift upwards into the Valencian sky. I think of my heart. It's all quiet on the phone. My Mum's voice appears softly saying, *I'd better go*, so I tell her I love her and she hang ups and the geezer with the black T-shirt and cherry red DMs looks away – he has been looking at me while I have been simultaneously listening to my Mum on the phone and looking at the Spanish kid feeling his heartbeat. I pull myself up from my chair and lift my glass and wave it towards him and nod at him, *d'ya wanna beer mate?* He smiles and his deep brown eyes light up and he replies back; *honest mate, I'll get them, it's nice to hear an English accent, I thought you were a local until your phone went.*

After I introduce myself, I sit back down. He tells me that his people call him Moon – originally from Brighton but now lives in Tennessee and he's over in Valencia for the week with work, and we shake hands and he asks me what I'm having and I explain to him I'm on the zero percent San Miguel, Doctor's orders, so he does an about-turn and heads into the restaurant to put the order in to the cute señorita with the large gold ear-rings and beautiful thick dark hair, braided perfectly in French plaits. In the shadows I can just about make Moon out – his hands rest on the counter – freshly polished dark brown wood – exquisite snacks and delicate delicacies display their glory behind the glass – a black board showing today's specials is elegantly written in coloured chalk – it offers the finest paella in the region – the famous seafood dishes of Spain. I sat firm on my seat and stood firm in my mind when Moon asked me what I'm having – it's another non-alcoholic Spanish beer, when really I want to savour a bottle of white wine; a rum and something; a single malt whiskey; a brandy and something; a jug of Sangria; a rich, red from the region – earlier Larry had a bottle of *El Angosto* – it means *The Narrow* – I raise my head to the sun and close my eyes letting the gold brightness spring-clean the dust in my brain, sweeping away dark clouds and leading me into a small garden of rich flowers and light, and when I open my eyes the waitress is clearing away Larry and I's empty plates of paella. I look at her but she's purposefully ignoring me. She doesn't look at me – I can feel her disdain for me glowing like the trace of a slug's trail – after Larry and I first sat down outside, I was admiring the hanging baskets of bright flowers adorning the outside of the shop, yellow petals and orange petals, I wondered if she watered them using a green watering can and watched the water drain through the soil and then drip down onto the concrete below. As I was wondering this, she bustled out the doorway and strode over to me pointing at the T-shirt in my hand while sneering at the naked upper half of my body. She furiously demanded that I had to put my shirt on or I'd risk an arrest. I apologised and obliged. She stormed back into her establishment as I sat down in bemused laughter. I wondered if Juan Mata had ever sat here outside this place. He signed for Valencia in 2007 and stayed there until last August when he signed for Chelsea – what a great little player – you can tell as well that he's one of the humble ones – he'll be up against it tomorrow tonight with Barca's midfield but they hate playing us and we're one-nil up and if the ref isn't on the take like Anders Frisk and Tom Henning Øvrebø were, then we've got a chance. Moon sits down in the chair that Larry vacated and I turn slightly to the side and cross my right leg over my left thigh, say thank you to Moon and ask him what he's doing on the streets of Valencia on his own and buying a stranger a drink and he smiles and tells me: *I got the drinks in, you go first and tell me why you're outside this café in the old town area of Valencia on a Monday afternoon so far from London.*

I smile while looking into his wide, brown eyes and explain to him that I'm getting a train to Barcelona in a couple of hours, or once my pal Larry comes back from his stroll around the old town – he's been gathering his thoughts – and then we've got Chelsea tomorrow night and, to be honest, I've packed up my troubles and bought them with me, but that's ok, they are piled up like dirty plates in a sink – well maybe a few will get washed while I'm here – I feel lighter already – so the cleaning has begun, and I imagine I'll sleep on the train, it's three hours or more to Barcelona, and I get tired man, really tired – like I could sleep for a week, and he nods like he understands and he sips from his bottle of beer and savours the taste, I offer him a cigarette and he declines and I prompt him, *your turn*, and he looks to the skies and runs his right hand over his freshly shaved head and says the name: *Wilf McFinnigan* and fixes a grin at me, and I reply: *What a brilliant name*, and he responds: *Yeah, good old Wilf McFinnigan*. Moon rests back in his seat and tells me:

I met him at a bar. Isn't that always how a good story starts? Once a week I was playing bass guitar in a band in a bar in Nashville and he was in another band playing keys. We would chat each time we met, we didn't know each other that well, but we did chat each time our paths crossed, maybe once a week or twice a month – you know how it is. I left England years before to emigrate with my wife, who's American. Then my wife left me. Wilf knew my wife had left me. I knew he had a farm – seventeen acres to be exact – and he rings me up and I let it go to answerphone and later on when I listened his voicemail, I knew I had to accept his offer, his words went through me – well, cut through me I suppose– like when you smash a lump of steak with a rolling pin – *bang!* – I've got a mate who does it with a baseball bat – flatten the meat, tenderise it – *wham!* – Wilf was like, *I'm out the country for four months, will you look after my farm please?* – and I knew I had to look after his farm, that it was the right thing to do.

Moon is silent now. I take my bottle and pour the amber liquid into a fresh glass. I ask him where Wilf was off to, for four months, going on tour or something? Moon smiles and explains that Wilf McFinnigan wasn't off on a tour, he was going to Haiti to look after orphans because of an earthquake and then Moon looks at me with those wide, brown eyes and says, *your turn then*, and I blow smoke out the corner of my mouth and admit, *I knew you were a musician*, and I ponder on picking up where I left off, though I'm not even sure where I left off – I reach for the ashtray and pull it closer to me and then I move my phone away from the edge to the middle of the table next to a small vase with some pretty yellow flowers in and I wonder when the last time was I bought flowers for Josie, I must buy her some flowers, maybe it'll do more damage, you know, the gesture will only paper over the cracks and cause more tension and more stress in the long run and encourage the wall between us to crack even further – or maybe the gesture will do the opposite – it will fill the cracks with love and forgiveness and courage and beauty and determined reconciliation.

I tell Moon that I'm signed off work, and I probably won't go back, my employer is looking at redundancy and that'll be best for everyone. The Doctor put me on these tablets to help me sleep – he asked me to go away and draw up a time-line of when my insomnia began – see if I can trace the route back to a root cause – and I go away and do this and it's been thirteen gruelling years since I slept through the night – even seven years ago when I went to Australia for two months I couldn't sleep through the night – and each morning I got up and got on with it, but now I'm done – something's fractured in my mind – everything is dark and I hate that it is like that – I hate the words that are coming out of my mouth, but I'll never see you again, Moon, so what does it matter how open I am with you? I found myself on the aeroplane this morning thinking that I didn't care if it went down. What sort of prick thinks that? I've got a wife and two beautiful kids at home, parents who love me and some proper, decent mates. My head is screwed up, man. So, please tell me about this farm, I'm not sure I want to talk about me, I want to listen to you, I'm bored of my own voice, bored of all this shit, bored of not being able to have a drink because of these meds, it's the second-leg of the semi-final of the European Cup and I can't have a drink – well, I could, but I'd probably end up passed out in the gutter when the alcohol collides with the medication, and that won't help me get better, will it? Moon responds; *sounds like you need to get better, day-by-day and all that*, and I nod in agreement and study the petals of the yellow flowers in the small vase in the middle of the table and say to Moon; *Right, so you looked after seventeen acres, then?*

Moon nods and says there were six goats, forty chickens and one cow. I interrupt and ask what the cow's name was, and he replies that Wilf didn't name the cow, because the cow was going to be slaughtered, and if you name the cow you begin a connection with the cow because it has a name, so it's just a cow. I interrupt Moon again by saying that if it's just a cow, isn't that still a name? I'm off to feed The Cow – you could call the cow Colin – I'm off to feed Colin the Cow surely has the same connection as I'm off to feed The Cow – and Moon says; *Mmmm, I hadn't thought of that*, and I reply; *don't tell Wilf McFinnigan and by the way, remind me to tell you about Colin the Cockerel later,* this makes Moon look quizzically at me, his eyes go wider still as he replies; *okay,* and then with my right hand I motion at him to continue, and so he does.

The goat needed milking twice a day. Udders and a bucket. And it took two days to mow the field. I was driving a tractor with this mowing contraption fixed on the back, blades rotating chopping up the green – felt like there was no end to the cycle. One time I'm driving the tractor around the field, cutting the grass, and I thought about digging my own grave. It came to me just like that – *I'm gonna dig my own grave.* My next thought was; *I'm gonna buy my own spade – a proper shovel –* so right there and then I drove the tractor around the front, got in my car and headed off to buy a massive shovel, but the hardware store was shut. I would have to go home and use a normal garden spade rather than the shovel I wanted to buy.

We both laugh. I picture him outside the hardware store all pissed off that the store was shut. I imagine the goat back on the farm with a full udder that needed milking, however Moon is stuck standing in front of a sign that says CLOSED. He continues:

So, I'm probably on an FBI hit-list somewhere, because I went back, fired up my laptop and looked up on the internet how to dig a grave for a human. It said it takes four to six hours to dig. I found a tape-measure, got a bottle of Lucozade and a giant chocolate bar. One of those quotes came up on the laptop screen: *'The people that are afraid of dying are afraid of living!'* I didn't know what I thought about that, I probably disagreed to be honest, but I knew I wanted to dig by hand with a spade, not use one of the diggers. It was something that I *had* to do. I stood in the barn and I could smell petrol. Outside it was quiet, I could only hear the sound of the birds. I thought about setting up my phone to record the experience – I was trying to tell the story for the adventure. I thought I'd get clarity and release by digging this grave.... but I was feeling more and more angry because I was a madman in a field digging a hole trying to find the meaning – the meaning *of* something or the meaning *for* something. I used Wilf's garden spade and I dug for four hours. The sun came up. Dawn had arrived. It gets very hot in Tennessee. I needed my grave to be six-foot deep. I knew, because of my research, if I hit rock I was in trouble. I was cross. Really angry, because my grave wasn't how I wanted it to be. It looked like a bowl, not rectangular like in the movies. I wanted it to look okay – I needed it to be six-feet deep but at five-and-a-half-feet, I hit rock. I was standing in it, shovelling over my head. In my mind, I had failed my mission. But – I had got this far. What was my next step? Should I lie in it? Should I bury something? Maybe bury my divorce decrees? What about my bass guitar? That felt too dramatic. It felt like I was creating a story and I didn't know what the story was.... So, I lay down. I stayed lying in it for twenty minutes. I was waiting for a revelation. There wasn't one. Oh – and it wasn't like I could bury myself. You can't bury yourself. I can't be in two places at once. I needed someone to bury me. And no-one was about.

Moon took his lager off the table and held it between in his hands, rolling it slightly where the bottle neck meets the curve. I looked around and realised the Spanish kid and his Mama in her lemon-yellow dress were long gone. So too was Larry. I wondered where he was. I looked at Moon, who was looking to his left, his bottle in his hand. I wondered if he was smelling the barn, or hearing the sound of the Tennessee bird-songs, or thinking about holding a goat's udder and splashing milk into a silver bucket, or recalling the feel of soil and rock under his back as he lay in his grave looking up at the heat of the sun and tasting sweat and earth on his tongue. I hoped he'd tell me what happened next. After about a minute, he did:

I climbed out of my grave. I looked down in it with a mixture of shame and achievement. And then I asked myself: What next? *What next?* I then realised I was done. Six hours of digging. I was exhausted – but I decided to fill it in. Yep – I was going to fill it in. I did, but I couldn't get it flat. It was this mound – I had to flatten it. So, I did, I flattened it. Then I went home, got changed and went to work. I was running the sound at a music venue. The next day, I had to mow the field. So back I went, to mow, and I was driving around and I drove over my mound. I hopped off the tractor, pulled out my penis…. And pissed on my grave.

Tears now filled those brown eyes of his. And then he started laughing. He wiped his face with the back of his hand and I started laughing too. He reached for his bottle and lifted it up. I raised my glass and we clinked our drinks together. We held them there for a couple of seconds, his brown bottled glass on my clear white glass, and then he pulled his hand away and was the first of us to drink, he put the bottle to his lips and drank it all the way down. I raised my glass to my lips and did the same.

All right, lads?

Larry is back with a big grin on his face. I introduce Moon who stands and shakes Larry's hand. Larry says *nice to meet you, Moon* and then looks at me and reminds me we've got a train to catch then adds he's gonna have a quick piss. He disappears through the shadowy door; I imagine him looking for the sign to the Gents. Now he's returned from his walk I pick up my phone off the table, turn it off and put it in my rucksack. I'll try not to turn it on again until I land back at Gatwick on Wednesday morning. Moon asks me about the story of Colin the Cockerel. I laugh and tell him my mate Geoff was doing some work for a local rag, there was an anti-social behavioural order put on a cockerel for crowing too loudly, it was such a bizarre story, all the nationals picked up on it, and Geoff got a few quid out of it, but it was a couple of years ago now. Moon asks if Geoff is a journalist, I said he dabbled for a bit, but now he's gone back working for his Dad's firm tarmacking roads. Moon says he'll google it – I tell him if the FBI is tracking his searches, they'll have a right laugh reading about a cock making too much noise in the Hampshire countryside. He puts out his hand, I shake it and he clamps his other hand on top of mine. His skins feel rough. Bass player hands. Farmers fingers. I thank him for the drink, he says it was his pleasure, I say I might write about this one day, and he says be my guest. He takes his hand away, rises from his chair and pats me on the shoulder.

I reach for my packet of cigarettes as Moon starts walking away. I stand up and watch him go. I look at his cherry red DMs, strolling all the way up the street, pedestrians only, and as I'm about to turn my back to go in the opposite direction, he turns around and stops, hands on his hips. Then he stretches his arms high in the air and begins to wave. He doesn't wave in the standard way, he criss-crosses them back and forth, while walking backwards. He's too far away for me to make out any features, but I know he is smiling. I wave back the same way too, it's just how my Gran would from her third-floor balcony, criss-crossing her arms, waving goodbye, I'd watch her from the window of the car as a kid until my Dad had driven around the corner and she was out of sight – suddenly Moon is out of sight, too. I stop waving and look down to see a business card on the floor by my right foot, I bend down and pick it up – it's a business card from this place – I shove it in the back right pocket of my jeans. I feel a bit hollow and vacant, like Moon has pecked me on the cheek and then ridden off on his horse like a lone cowboy. Then I think maybe I'm the needy teenage girl, craving attention. I picture what I think Wilf McFinnigan might look like, sitting in the dust with grieving Haitians surrounded by their rubble, hearts cracking, dust soaking up their tears. I pull my orange lighter out of my pocket and spark up another cigarette.

Chapter Three

BARCELONA

Monday 23rd April 2012

I span around in child-like wonder, there were single men dotted everywhere holding single red roses. Larry is looking at a map on the wall of the immediate vicinity, I'm spinning slowly and deliberately, spotting red roses in palms, some wrapped in cellophane, some not, all in contrast to the yellow and orange petals in the Valencian hanging baskets, it must be Valentine's Day over here or something – Saint Valentine – a martyr – *and now these three remain: faith, hope and love; but the greatest of these is love.* Some sort of Catalan tradition, I expect. Now one, then two, then three women in my vision greet their men, an embrace here to my right, a tentative hug there a bit further on, a kiss and a spin to my left – my gaze stays on this third couple as they kiss and spin, spin and kiss – Larry calls my name and peels away from the map on the wall, says the Hotel is only round the corner and up the road a bit, I step in time next to him and I smile and nod at an elderly man holding a red rose wondering if his sweetheart is coming up the escalator to greet him.

The train journey took three hours, Larry had a four-pack to keep him going, I sat transfixed at times at the view, my forehead occasionally banging on the window as the train lurched and hugged the coastline, jagged rock and that brochure blue sky and sea once again laid out before me. When the view became more urban I wanted to keep my eyes open but they closed and I stretched out and I realised there were no shadows and no snow, no darkness and no fuzziness, I don't know how long I dozed for, it wasn't a deep sleep, I remember realising my mouth was open and my mouth was dry, I'd probably been drooling. In a fragmented dream I pictured looking over my shoulder at my children in their car seats fast asleep and not being able to keep my eyes off them as they snoozed – out for the count – Josie placing her hand on my thigh and just resting it there as she drove us home, the mother of my children, I hear her gentle voice pleading *don't talk like that* as big tears fell from her sad., fearful eyes as I pulled away like a robot without a heart, the meds knocking me for six, I don't know who I am anymore, imagine going to bed and contemplating if it would be a release for all concerned to not wake up, I'd be at peace and eventually Josie would find hers, but I did wake up and as long as I continue to wake up each morning I'd better get my shit together. Here I am at the Hotel reception front desk watching more men scattered around the foyer holding single red roses, they're everywhere, and suddenly Larry is being served, so I turn to concentrate.

The plump, jovial fellow handing us the keys to our room looks like the Fat Controller in Thomas the Tank Engine. It reminds me of my son, three years old, sitting at the dinner table, me picking up his spoon with some beans and mash on and explaining to him he needs to finish his food: *Here comes Thomas into the tunnel!* And he replies *choo-choo* and opens his mouth wide, I pop the spoon in and he eats. The thought of him makes me want to hold him, to blow raspberries on his neck, hear him laugh, lift him up under his armpits and place him on my shoulders, grip his ankles with my hands to keep him steady as we walk, feel his hands on my hair and listen to him sing. The Fat Controller asks us about the purpose of our trip, smoothing down his mustard waistcoat holding in his rotund belly under a white shirt, an unbuttoned black suit matching his black bow-tie. All that was missing was a top hat. Larry tells him Chelsea are going to win the European Cup and he beams at us: *oh! Bueno! Bueno! Here for football!* Then he asks us if we have any questions and I've got my swimming shorts in my rucksack so I ask him what time the pool opens, (Larry was delighted when he booked the Hotel, he told me there was a roof-top pool and since then I've been picturing myself lying in it and doing a length or two and then sipping from my over-priced bottle of mineral water as I drip-dried on a white plastic sun lounger), and the front desk clerk cocks his head to one side and says: *repeat please*, so I point upwards and repeat: *what time does the swimming pool open, please?* The cheery Fat Controller chap spreads his hands on the desk, his fingers like plump butcher's sausages, he looks at Larry who is excited and expectant, got that soppy grin over his chops, the Fat Controller tries unsuccessfully to suppresses a chortle. He takes his sausage fingers off the desk, holds his stomach and starts to giggle. He looks back to me and announces: *IN JUNE!* All three of us burst out laughing. As we take the stairs up to our level I mutter through my smiles that I cannot believe the roof-top pool opens in bloody June and Larry bemoans the situation – *of course it's April, it's out of season* – and reiterates how much he was looking forward to it, being up on the roof with a swimming pool, and we both burst out laughing again. I imagine the Fat Controller telling a colleague behind the front desk what just happened and laughing some more.

Our beds are separated by a table, I take the bed by the window because when Larry stays out later than me tonight his bed is closer to our door when he comes back. I lie on my bed in only my boxer shorts while he showers. I think about hanging up my smart polo that I'm wearing tomorrow, but I can't be bothered. Next thing I know is I've got my forehead against the wall and the hot shower water is blasting onto my neck and my hands are placed on the wall too, palms up either side of the showerhead, I look down to the plug hole and the water spinning away, rushing out of sight, I picture the third couple I spotted at the train station greeting each other with red roses and spinning and kissing and I picture the hanging baskets in Valencia dripping water on to concrete, petals of orange and yellow, and I imagine the roof-top pool up above me, all empty of water, just a crater of blue tiles and grey concrete – in the corner the white sun loungers are stacked plastic on top of plastic, I wonder how Moon is and what he's doing now, and I see myself sitting on the edge of the pool at Dancing Ledge with my legs dangling in the water and then Larry is knocking on the door urging me out; *let's go mate* and I go to tell him that I don't even remember him getting out the shower and me getting in, but I think better of it, I turn off the shower and watch the water drip off my body for a bit and scratch my ear with my little finger, squelch the water out one ear and then the other, wonder where the time went, wonder how long I zoned out for, can't remember getting in here, overwhelmingly grateful for Larry's company, though.

Larry has been to Barcelona before with his cousin Seagull Si, and I'm happy to walk where he leads. The only thing I'm worried about is making sure I get an early night and take my meds, I don't mind Larry kicking on, he always does, we were up at Bolton one year and we'd been drinking since the morning and me and George were shattered, we were in a Travelodge and it had been a Saturday three o'clock kick off, we'd all been for a massive curry. I'd had a shower and I was in bed with my book, an Elmore Leonard one. George had the TV on – he told me he had to watch X-

Factor because when he got home the next day, his young daughter would want to talk all about it – so with that Larry announced to us that he was going back off out on his own, and he ended up in a pub where there was a Billy Connolly tribute act, he told us all about it on the drive home the next morning, he's one of these drinkers that can keep going, I can't, my lights go out, and that was all before being on this medication, anyway.

Now, I sit outside a place that Larry chooses while he goes inside for the drinks. I take my cigarettes out of the breast pocket of my fresh shirt and look around at the early evening scene, people are dotted around, this is nice, Larry puts down a San Miguel zero percent in front of me and says that a couple of the lads who drink in the Fox in Putney are inside, so he ducks back in. I pour some of the drink in my glass and start to feel hungry and then a wave of nausea comes from nowhere, I put my lit cigarette in the ashtray, push back my chair and get my head low, as low as I can.

I stay in this position, backside right on the edge of my chair with my head between my knees, the giddiness has passed but feel I pins and needles in my fingers, I waggle them by my sides, they are numb. I raise my head gingerly and see my cigarette has burned right to its end, white menthol butt still wedged in the groove of the ash tray. I straighten my back and click my neck, re-adjust my posture in the chair and notice on the pavement a deeply tanned Gypsy boy with thick clumps of black hair is standing next to his sister – as I look up, they look away. I instinctively know they are siblings because she is lent into her brother for protection or for intimacy or for comfort – I know this because it is how my daughter leans into her brother – and the more I look at them studying me, the more I reckon they're twins. The boy reaches his arm behind his back and pulls out a small tube – he pulls the end of the tube and it extends – I realise it's a telescope – he holds it to his eye the wrong way round while pointing it towards the orange trees down the street and starts laughing – he says something through his giggles to his sister and hands over the telescope to her – she takes it and puts it to her eye the correct way round and her brother laughs a no and takes it off her, turns it back around so it's the wrong way round and gives it back to her. She starts to giggle, which sets him off again, their laughter is infectious, looking at an orange tree that has been made tiny, (because the telescope is the wrong way round), it quickens my heart – I feel it under my shirt in this moment – and I wonder if I've been looking through my lens the way that makes everything small, I need to turn it around and see things as they should be, rebuild my world on my family, refocus on what I want in life, yeah – turn the telescope around the way it should be. The girl hands the telescope back to her brother who returns it to his back pocket and they turn to face each other and nod to each other and then skip off and I'm left in a void and it occurs to me that when I was bent over they were probably staring at me through their telescope, thinking I was a drunk Englishman slumped with his head low between his knees, and then turning their telescope around to spy on me all small and insignificant and then Larry appears and says he's well hungry and I respond *I'm famished, mate.*

Crossing a square there are people intermittently offering us business cards in an attempt to usher us into their establishment and Larry talks to one lady with crazy, corkscrew hair, sun-glasses perched on the top of her head, the hearty, natural laugh of an extrovert and an admission that she's on commission. Larry takes her card and asks for another one for me. I hear him with a twinkle in his voice say: *Carla, I promise you we'll go there after dinner,* I laugh that she's told him her name, that personal touch, and her accent is as beautiful as her dark skin when she flirts slightly: *Make sure you bring your friend with you, Larry* – and this makes me instinctively wave at her as Larry hands me one of the business cards she gave him and I place it in the back right pocket of my jeans. Dinner is two bottles of mineral water and a half-pound burger and large fries and a ton of salad, Larry has two pints and a steak with chips and salad and now he's got a thirst on, a night out in Barcelona awaits, I pay the bill with cash and leave a tip and the waiter takes a photo of both of us, it's the first photo we've had, we shake hands with the waiter and then out we go, the evening is colder now, the wind has picked right up, I'm glad I've got my jacket, once again I step in time with Larry and for the first time I notice he has a new pair of Stan Smiths on. While admiring them a distinctive sound cuts right through us, teasing us on the breeze – we turn to look at each other, Larry looks the happiest I've seen him, a weight has come off him. We can hear where we are going before we can see the venue, Carla wasn't lying, the unmistakable anthem, the best song in the world, the reason we are here, the reason we do the things that we do, it carries on the wind: *Chelsea! Chelsea! Chelsea! Chelsea! Chelsea! Chelsea! Chelsea!*

We step through the open door with our arms aloft, there's about sixty Chelsea to our left and ten or so standing at the bar to our right and most of them look over as one as we've walked in off the street and I punch the air in time: *Chelsea! Chelsea! Chelsea!* Larry sings as he steps up to the bar, both of his long arms in the air as strangers pat him on the back vociferous: *Chelsea! Chelsea! Chelsea!* I scan around and I don't recognise anyone, the lads from Putney still back at that other place, maybe. I move to the side of the bar and position myself by an empty stool, standing for now, and watch Larry pull out Carla's business card, the barman has his back to Larry, it's adorned with palm trees, it's a proper Hawaiian shirt he's peacocking, he's sorting out something by the till, he's got a red hat on his head, like a joke fez number that Tommy Cooper would wear, dark curls sticking out from the back and sides, once he turns around he smiles jovially at Larry with Catalan eyes, his pencil moustache twitching, clocks the business card and beams: *ten percent off first drinks!* I can't hear Larry but I work out he's talking about spirits. The barman shows him a goblet and Larry makes a shape with his hands saying *bigger?* and the barman laughs and reaches up above his head, slightly on tip-toes, and brings down an even bigger goblet and the barman fills it with ice and points at the various bottles of rum until Larry instructs *stop, yes please, that one* and the barman carries the bottle of rum over to me, putting it on the top of the bar. I give him my order as he tips the bottle over the ice, it makes a satisfying gurgling as the rum continues oozing out and the *Chelsea! Chelsea! Chelsea!* seems to be in time with the *glug glug glug* of the golden rum pouring out the bottle and the singing feels like it goes up a notch, more determination this time, like the other year up at Anfield, two years ago next month, our pre-match battlecry drowning out their shit and everyone in the away end has got goose-bumps. *Chelsea! Chelsea! Chelsea!*

When the song finally stops, there is a raucous round of applause, and as that dies down this younger fella, got to be eighteen to twenty years-old, he is sat at a table in the open plan restaurant at the back, now he's up standing on his chair and he's got a West Ham top on, bloody hell, this could end badly. Everyone jeers at him, but the lad is full of Dutch Courage. I wait for the atmosphere to change but that switch doesn't get flicked, he starts singing *bubbles* and he only gets the first line out: *I'm forever blowing bubbles* and then everyone joins in, slowly like it should be sung, old Shed boys and bench boys all in here with pints in the air and Larry holds up his giant goblet of rum, coke and ice towards the lad and I do likewise with my glass of zero percent – all the Chelsea serenade him with their glasses aloft looking straight at him, *pretty bubbles in the air, they fly so high, they reach the sky, and like West Ham they fade and die! Tottenham always running, Arsenal running too. We're the Chelsea boot boys and we're running after you! Chelsea! Chelsea!* The West Ham lad is laughing in disbelief, no idea Chelsea had their own version, and he raises his pint back shaking his head in surrender knowing he should've known better, now his girlfriend is pulling him down off the chair all embarrassed, and then as one everyone puts their drink down and applauds the guy and his poor partner, the waiter hovering nearby exhales dramatically, he's seen it all before, and pencil moustache behind the bar raises an eyebrow like Carlo Ancelotti does and then someone starts a song I've never heard before and I absolutely love it; *Thank you very much for Frankie Lampard! Thank you very much, thank you very, very, very much! Thank you much for Frankie Lampard! Thank you very much, thank you very, very, very much!* And everyone is laughing, the West Ham lad's girlfriend has got her head in her hands, and Larry asks me if I remember that advert for Roses chocolates with that jingle, which I do, so we both smile and sing: *Thank you very much you're one in a million, thank you very much, thank you very, very, very much! Thank you very much for feeding William, thank you very much, thank you very, very, very much!* We both laugh remembering the advert, William was a goldfish and whoever fed William got a box of Roses as a thank you, I think it was a bespectacled kid. The West Ham fan and his girlfriend have paid their bill and start their walk of shame from the open restaurant section at the back of the gaff along the bar towards the exit, front door still open. He gets a couple of sporting pats on the back and they're both a little uncomfortable but smiling and Larry reaches over and says *Cheers mate, have a good holiday* and I raise my glass to him, the girlfriend is looking at the floor and he is just laughing taking it all in his stride, all good natured, and then someone bellows *Where's your famous ICF?* and then they're out the door, gone.

I drain my glass but the thing is with these zero percent beers is that after a few I get a bitter aftertaste in my mouth like when I was a kid when I've licked a two pence-piece, or as a teenager when I've walked into the bathroom straight after my big sister has covered her head with cheap Woolworths hairspray. The barman comes over and asks *same again?* I order a Coke for me, but the same again for Larry, he nods, his pencil moustache twitching, his Hawaiian shirt hanging loosely off his shoulders, he has a name badge on that reads *BONGOJO,* as he turns I instinctively clock desolation or regret in his eyes, don't know why, it's a sense, something intuitive, so I call after him to have one himself and he turns back and grins over his shoulder – *Sí! Estrella! Gràcies!* – he bowed his head slightly before reaching up for a clean, giant goblet for Larry's rum. Someone calls towards us: *See ya later, fellas,* a few of the Chelsea boys are filing out, three or four at first, then more, I turn my back to look out the window over my shoulder and a pack of cigarettes is being offered around, then another five or six lads follow and Larry says *Up the Chels* and a couple of defiant fists are shaken our way: *This is it, lads,* and an *Up the fuckin' Chels* follows and one of them looks to the corner and orders, *Deano, Al, Tim – let's go,* they nod back, more file past us and then off they walk to their next place, a good thirty of them, and with the front door still open I hear a: *You Are My Chelsea, my only Chelsea!* as the group walk away. BongoJo puts our drinks down and I fish a ten Euro out my pocket and ask him it it's enough, he says *yes, yes,* and I sit down on the stool and Larry says he's going for a piss and then out for a smoke.

BongoJo places some loose change with a receipt down on a small terracotta coloured saucer in front of me, thanks me for the drink and offers his hand which I shake. He points to his name badge and tells me I can call him Jo. He asks me when I flew in, I said to Valencia this morning and he says *ah, then the train?* And I say *yeah, train* and then I ask him why, at the train station, did so many people have single red roses – is it Valentine's Day or something? And Jo cocks his head and his pencil moustache twitches and I expand further, telling him there were more men with roses in the Hotel foyer and as I've walked around tonight, there's people with single red roses, always a single red rose and he responds, *yes, yes,* and spreads his hands on the bar, his Hawaiian shirt sleeves are rolled up to the elbow, his fingers beneath the knuckles are hairy and the hair gets thicker on the back of his hand and thicker still travelling up his arm, an indistinguishable tattoo sticks out from his left shirt sleeve, I can smell his after-shave, he explains: *Today ees a Saint George day – the patron Saint of Catalonia! Sant Jordi!* I listen to Jo explain about their patron Saint. In my mind I figure it's a romantic blend of our St. George's Day and Valentine's Day, a mixture rolled together, a brave knight killing a Dragon and saving the Princess, and the thing that sticks out most to me in the tale he is telling me is that, according to legend, a red rose sprouted from the blood of the dragon – this is where the tradition was born, presenting a rose to a woman.

As I reflect on this, Jo moves to the length of the bar to serve someone and now the pine for alcohol is strong in me, I fight it back by closing my eyes and picturing my Josie holding our daughter who has pulled up Josie's top slightly and is kissing Josie's tummy and saying: *Baby! Baby!* She does this because her brother, my son, is growing inside. Opening my eyes, I find myself looking by the till right where Jo has the drink I bought him and lying by the bottle is a single red rose, it lies redundant, Jo's partner nowhere to be seen, maybe this is why sadness reigns behind his pupils. Larry calls my name as he steps through the open door and blowing smoke out of the side of his mouth he asks if we should have one more here and I reply *do you mind if you walk me back?* and he says course he doesn't and explains he'll go back out once I'm settled in and I say *I know* with a smile and he puts one of his long arms around my shoulders and pulls me into him and shouts *Up the Chels!* and pushes me away laughing. I call out to Jo and wave a goodbye, turning to leave. I take a cigarette out my pack and offer Larry one and he screws his nose up because they're menthol and then says *oh go on then* and my legs feel tired, the drink of Coke has made my teeth feel all furry, and the sedatives will cause me to sleep long and hard, I know I won't even hear Larry when he comes back later, and that is a miracle, I tell you, the Doctor wasn't wrong putting me on these pills and signing me off.

As I lie on my bed in my boxer shorts in the dark staring at the ceiling, I hear Larry flush the toilet and then turn the bathroom light off. I close my eyes as he softly closes the door behind him to go back out to paint the town red. Then the visions began.

Chapter Four

HOTEL DREAMS

Monday night / Tuesday morning

Someone is in the square by the orange trees crouched under a giant red fez, must be a contortionist of sorts. Princess Carla, (the beautiful dark-skinned young lady with the corkscrew curls dishing out business cards for ten percent off our first drinks), is in a royal medieval dress, her bosoms pushed tight together by a corset, she is tied to an orange tree with thick rope. A petit, golden crown balances on her pretty curls and I hear Jesus: *Be faithful even to the point of death, and I will give you the crown of life.* Music is playing and people are clapping, everyone has secured red roses under their armpits as they clap, when the music quickens so does the clapping, and crawling out from under the red fez, unwinding himself, even – is the Fat Controller! He's dressed as a pantomime Dragon and he bellows out a song, an opera of sorts, and then Carla responds by singing her woes about her impending virginal, untimely death, tossing her head to the side, her corkscrew curls swaying about, her chest expanding with the music – now as the Dragon approaches the Princess a trumpet sounds and through the cheers of the delighted crowd Jo, (as Saint George), appears in splendid armour on a horse made out of two wheels either side of a broom stick, the head made out of papier-mâché or something, he stops and sings for a bit offering out the Dragon all dramatically and heroic, his pencil moustache twitching. This prompts the Fat Controller Dragon to sing back. Princess Carla wails in distress, St. George waves a sword above his head, the silver foil covering it flashes in the sun, he sinks the foil sword under the Fat Controller's arm pit who makes a big deal about slowly dying. Then St. George takes the sword out and a huge red rose blossoms in its place. St. George plunges the sword heroically into the Dragon's other arm pit and then he takes the red rose that appeared and puts the green stalk in his mouth and the Fat Controller breathes his last and flops to the floor with an operatic climax. The crowd whoops with joy at the slain beast. Moving and singing his way over to the

Princess, our saintly hero cuts the ropes free and embraces Carla, his love, and they kiss to the cheers of the crowd and to end it all, this big crescendo of noise plays, and the two lovers twirl and hug and spin around and spin around and hug and hug and spin around and spin around and hug as the jubilant crowd reigns down applause.

Now I'm outside sitting on a chair with my head between my knees, I slowly raise my head and I look up to see a deeply tanned Gypsy boy with thick clumps of black hair standing next to his sister – I instinctively know they are siblings because she is lent into her brother for protection or for intimacy or for comfort – I reckon they're twins – the boy reaches his arm behind his back and pulls out a small tube – he pulls the end of the tube and it extends – I realise it's a telescope – and he passes it to me. His sister is practically hidden by her mass of black, messy hair – she starts giggling at me and motions at me to put the telescope to my eyes, and she points down the road, I follow to where she is pointing with my eye-line, but I can't make anything out so I look back at her and shrug my shoulders. She grins showing me missing front teeth and motions at me to put the telescope to my eyes, and I do and everything is small and tiny and the boy and girl burst out laughing and jabber something in their native tongue and together they take the telescope from me, turn it around and place it back in my hands. They both point together down the street, down the promenade, showing me which direction to look at, so now I look the correct way down the telescope. I had to turn it around to observe things as they should be, and I gasp at what I see.

I see my bedroom in my old flat, it is displayed like a doll's house, like when it opens up and you can move figures about and swap miniature furniture around. There is blood on the white bed sheet and I start to feel a little faint, it appears as if burgundy has been spilt on the sheets – panic bubbles, but then I'm reassured because I notice the bottle of gas and air by the side of the bed, I can see the midwife is stitching up Josie, her knees are apart, her legs are spread and she's looking up at the ceiling and the midwife is moving in, looking in closer and talking about a possible fractured pelvis, so I purposefully move the telescope slightly to the left away from that personal, private procedure and I see myself sitting on my bedroom floor in only a pair of shorts, I'm bare chested and I'm cradling my newborn girl, just holding her and I feel my tears fall as I watch myself holding her, they told me that skin-on-skin is important, I've been talking to my baby for months as she grew in the womb, and now I can't keep my eyes off of myself not being able to keep my eyes off her, and I can't tell how long I sat there in real life or how long I watched a re-run of this from peering down the telescope but I can hear my voice saying: *thank you, God, oh thank you, Jesus* in relief and praise and wonder, then I whisper *I LOVE YOU* into the skin of my child. When I take my eye away from the telescope the Gypsy twin children are waiting with their hands in the pockets, heads cocked to one side, fascinated. I hold the telescope out and when the girl goes to take it, I snatch it back smiling and both twins laugh. I hold my palm up to signal *wait* while I fish in my pocket and take out some change. I hand the little girl a two Euro coin and gently ruffle her thick mane, and then return the telescope to her. The little boy holds out a mucky palm, dirt thick under long nails, and I place a two Euro coin in the centre of his hand and ruffle his black shock of hair – they both hold their respective coins up to the sky as if it were treasure, then skip off down the long road with glee.

I stand up and stretch and see Moon walking towards me and he announces proudly that it's his round. I follow him into a boozer called *MUSIC CITY BLUES* where neon lights flash *NASHVILLE TENNESSEE* at me in pink and green. Moon nods at the barman who takes a large bottle of red wine and two glasses. Moon tells me this is where he watches Chelsea games, gestures at the barman and says he's had the wine imported from Valencia and I study the label and it says *EL ANGOSTO* in Spanish which means *THE NARROW* and Moon smiles and instructs me: *You're asleep now, you can have a drink, you deserve it* and I say to him: *This is what Larry was drinking earlier, was it?* And Moon goes, *yeah, it is – I thought you'd like that* and then I talk to Moon about the birth of my daughter, and then he tells me all about the birth of his first daughter and as we exchange heart-felt stories the only thing that interrupts me is a young lad in a West Ham top blowing bubbles from a pot – he holds a plastic stick with a hole at each end, dips one end in the pot to soak it in bubble mixture and then places it near his mouth and gently blows. The bubbles float over the bar and the two Gypsy twins jump up to catch the bubbles and when I look down I notice there's a single red rose in my hand and the thorn has cut my finger and there's blood dripping down my palm and tracing a line down my arm and the blood is just like the blood from the Fat Controller's armpit; the blood is just like the blood on the white sheets in Josie and I's bed; the blood is just like the blood from a home-birth – in true Catalan tradition, sprouting from the blood forms a single red rose, just like the red in my large glass, I clink mine with Moon's, put the blood red wine to my lips and take a generous mouthful. Moon says to me: *When you're at the end of yourself, that's when you find yourself* and I nod and restudy the wine bottle, carefully reading the label again, *EL ANGOSTO* and then I hear Jesus: *Enter through the narrow gate. For wide is the gate and broad is the road that leads to destruction, and many enter through it. But small is the gate and narrow the road that leads to life, and only a few find it.*

I try and stand up to stretch but I'm buckled into my seat. I look into my lap at the metal silver clasp and the black fabric of the seat belt holding me firm. Looking to my right, I study Larry who is in the window seat. He's leaning forward with his forehead resting against the back of the seat in front. I can't discern the names of the weights that sit heavy on his shoulders, but I can see their shapes pushing down on his large frame, they are changing the whole form of his posture, his back is bent, his knees straining under the pressure, his forehead light with mild sweat – I picture grabbing the shape in a headlock, its demonic form squirms and kicks back against my firm grip, it's under my right armpit – I hold the shape firm in a headlock – its evil configuration grows wrists and hands and tries to heave itself out of my clutches to slip away to escape but I'm too strong – in my left hand I hold the gold, magic lamp as heavy as a brick, and I'm cracking it again and again on to the head of the demonic shape and I'm screaming at it to fuck off and die and get off my pal, *stop weighing him down,* I open the emergency exit and fling it out into oblivion, it screeches far below out of sight, out of mind, defeated and beaten, its shape returns to Hell where it burns to oblivion.

I stand up and stretch looking out over Dancing Ledge – there's the kid from Valencia who had discovered his heartbeat sitting on his Mama's lap and he's crying. The Mother is trying to soothe him but he lets out a louder wail. She looks at me and arches her eyebrows, switches her son to rest on her other thigh, lemon yellow summer dress hitching up her leg. Smoothing the material back down she talks over her sniffling son in broken English: *he thaid to me that he don't want he'th heart to thstop,* I cock my head to one side and repeat: *He said to you that he doesn't want his heart to stop?* She laughs with resignation: *He don't want mine to thstop eeethar.* It dawns on me that the penny has dropped in his head – his heartbeat keeps him alive, his Mama too, the person he loves more than anything else in the world –

and one day his heart will stop, mine too, yours too – the poor little man. I step over and bend down and look to him, his Mama shifts her body slightly, the hem of her lemon yellow dress dancing in the slight breeze – I reach out my hand and whisper: *Vamos*, and he turns his head to me and I nod towards the pool and he says: *Frio?* And I confirm: *Si, és frio – cold!* and he laughs and wipes his nose with the back of his hand and shuffles off the comfort of the lemon yellow, puts a pair of diving googles on, the elastic snaps on to the back of his head scrunching his hair, he adjusts the curved plastic over his eyes and takes my hand. We step on rock. Standing at the edge I admire that brochure blue sky that's our backdrop and he counts down: *Tres! Dos! Uno!* and we jump in, collide with sharp water, heartbeats increasing instantaneously with the rush, my clogged arteries taking a deserved kicking, I feel my heart pounding with shock and I stay right down there as long as I can, and then it was all quiet around me.

I open my eyes all startled and panicky because I momentarily think that I might be drowning – I look around, I don't know where I am, and then I hear Larry calling my name as he draws the curtains letting the daylight into our Hotel room. He's fully dressed and he throws me a packet of sandwiches, grinning, it lands on my torso and he says in imperfect Spanish: *Queso and jamón bocadillo-sandwich, mate!* And I smile and together we exclaim: *CHEESE SANDWICH!* It is one of our private jokes, we went up Middlesbrough one year, Taxi Alan driving, and we pull over at a service station and Larry goes: *Do you want a cheese sandwich or something?* Taxi Alan just jovially shouted back at him: *Cheese sandwich!* And we all cracked up and now it's a catchphrase. Larry explains that he came in after two o'clock and I was spark out – I say I didn't hear him come in and that's a good thing, and he says he woke up hungry so went for a walk to eat breakfast and bought me that snack back, and I ask him what the time is and he replies that it's about eleven and I mumble: *Man, these sedatives are strong* and Larry pointed at me all serious and said: *You need those meds in your life mate, you need to get better,* and then I started crying.

Larry sat on the end of his bed and stroked his chin, reached out to the table and pulled open the drawer. He fished out the match tickets for tonight's game. He waved them towards me with his toothy grin and placed them on top of the small television set. I smiled, sniffed and wiped my eyes with my hands and asked Larry to pass me the notepad and pen that were in the same drawer mixed in with our passports and the return train tickets to Valencia airport and the plane tickets to Gatwick and he said: *Sure, why?* And I replied: *I need to write down my dreams.*

Chapter Five

MIRACLE AT CAMP NOU

Tuesday 24th April 2012

Down at the marina you can feel the heat from the sun on your neck and your head and your arms; I'm indulged with a cacophony of scents; sea and salt, alcohol and suncream, flowers and salad dressing, tomatoes on the vine and the juice of freshly squeezed oranges. The laughter from the English lads ducks in and out on the breeze. Silver buckets full of chilled bottles of Estrella resting in crushed ice line the sparkling tables that stand on the dark, polished decking. To my right, a perfectly attired waiter with white gloves moves quickly, he carries a red crate of the local brew round to the front of the restaurant, brown bottles all clinking together as he angles the crate towards him, to my left there's a shout over the decking from one Londoner to another to order two more buckets from the bar while he's inside going for a piss.

Larry has ordered a massive seafood platter for the both of us to accompany our usual drinks. This place at the harbour is proper extravagant, but I'm never coming back here, putting my faith in redundancy pay arriving in June, we'll see. At the adjacent establishment, it seems to go up in price again. You can tell by the ropes cordoning off tables held by silver, polished clasps; the waiter with his silk cummerbund tight round his waist. He's holding a golden pen between his fingers. I subtlety watch the way the two female customers hold themselves opposite each other on an ample table for two in their expensive, colourful spring dresses and their shiny, olive skin. I admire the richness of their salon hair, notice the jewels on their fingers dripping luxuriousness. They take their time picking at their one hundred Euro starters that accompany their flutes of fine Dom Pérignon – when done they rise elegantly from their seats just like the bubbles in their tall-stemmed glasses. I wonder if they're going to stroll back to their yacht, I wonder if they are the partners of any of the Barcelona players. Not even an hour ago, while waiting to cross the road to come down to the harbour, the Barca team coach slowed to a halt in the traffic right in front of me. I stared at the blacked-out window a few feet away and mouthed *wankers* hoping that a snide like Messi or Fàbregas was looking straight back at me. Larry laughed.

The food is off the scale – chicken and seafood paella, locked and loaded with shrimp, clams, lobster, chorizo, rice, mussels – I don't know where to start, but start we do and the food is both savoured and demolished. After we're done, I twiddle with the business card accompanying the bill, all translated in English. One side explains how the restaurant offers a wide interpretation of the traditional market cuisine based on fish and seafood brought directly from the daily market fish. The other side states they offer an alternative explanation of traditional Spanish cuisine, with a clear penchant for fish and seafood of the highest quality. They couldn't decide what strapline to use, so they just used both, a different slogan on each side. As I pocket the card to keep as memorabilia, the early summer breeze rises, blowing in a freshness from the Balearic Sea, I could close my eyes right now and drift off, however, the arrival of more Chelsea to meet their gathered mates takes my attention instead.

Larry says he wants to stay for one more beer coz it's so lovely here, and I say sure and order a Coke. I light a cigarette and as I watch the smoke drift upwards into Catalonian sky and place my orange Clipper back on the table, four men take a seat adjacent to us, and they're polite and that, but I realise later on that was only because they wanted to taunt us about their adventures, look down on us as common muck, parade how they soak in their bath of indisputable wealth, a bank that will never run dry, the most expensive escort girls that money can buy, paid for their time and then paid for the intercourse. Each one of them are obese. Decked in shirts, trousers and shoes, they slobber over the menu and grunt private jokes at each other, in my thoughts I initially name them the four blokes of gluttony and then I settle on The Gluttonous Four. Gesticulating with his glass of white wine, the piggy nearest me with a jewel-encrusted gold ring stuck fast on his fat pinkie tells me that they travel the globe, no, *ride* the globe, to attend sporting events in corporate hospitality. He grunts with pride when he pronounces *ride*. He tells me they're here for the football, I imagine him gorging on his dinner, filling his face with extravagant desserts, and because he deduces that I'm not really engaging he takes that as a challenge, thinks maybe he has to impress me some more, find something he can boast about that I can relate to. He winks at me creepily when mentioning the young señorita last night sitting on his knee, and as he describes her, he grunts and grins when pausing to quaff his vino blanco. I have a flashback to the streets of Kenya, young girls and young boys orphaned and forced on the game, pimped to the highest bidder, it causes me to imagine taking his wine bottle out of the ice bucket neck first, smashing its base on the rail at the marina's edge, the jagged green glass flashing in the sun, returning to the table to Mr Piggy, slicing off his pinkie with my make-shift knife to set the suffocating ring free. I line up The Gluttonous Four against the harbour rail, tip crushed ice out of the silver bucket, watch it sparkle and start to melt on the edge of the marina. I order them to drop their wallets in the bucket, their watches, too. I flick the severed finger with the jewel off the table into the bucket. Got to be worth a few grand at least, that gem. I hand the lot to the señorita who was broken at his mercy last night and it somehow sets her free, heals her, she skips off to start a new life, swinging the bucket by her side, where there was darkness more than night, now she's shrouded in redemption, wrapped in wholeness while the piggy nonce, (who is lined up next to this three nonce mates), continues to holds his wrist in whimpering disbelief as blood pumps out of the hole in his fat hand where his sweaty little finger once lived.

Shaking away this daydream, I excuse myself to go for a piss, crossing the decking and moving into the bar to look for the Gents. There's a young lady with her back to the barman, elbows resting on the top of the bar, she oozes control, there is a guy either side of her, both leaning in, both thinking they're James Bond, dripping in Euros, Rolex's on their wrists, they're like putty, she's got them by the balls, she has an unlit cigarette between her fingers, neither of her admirers smoke, otherwise they would have offered her a light by now. Instinctively I put my hand to my pocket but I've left my orange Clipper on the table next to The Gluttonous Four, that would've been classic, little old me flicking my lighter to get her attention, her stepping forward and cupping the flame to light her cigarette, I smell coconut in her hair and moisturiser on her finger tips. I admire her surgeon-sculpted breasts plumped magnificently together, she touches my hand before stepping back, inhales her luxury cigarette, probably a *Treasurer,* and smiles a thank you, her lipstick bolder than my approach.

Sighing to myself at yet another daydream, I see the toilets to the rear of the bar. As I pass them, she touches one of her adoring men on the cheek with her free hand while looking at the other, (perhaps she is an actress), there is nothing like the intensity of a woman, she knows the power of her sexuality; she's got the two Catalan melts exactly where she wants them, panting like thirsty dogs, falling over each other like fools, I bet the barman can't look because he's so embarrassed by them.

Leaving the marina, Larry explains that one of The Gluttonous Four was telling him how they have an annual plan, the best hospitality money can buy, just been to the Malaysian Grand Prix, going to Monaco next month with the Italian, Abu Dhabi and Brazilian Grand Prix's all booked in. The choose Champions League games to go to, plus horse-racing and that. I tell Larry I hope they've got a private jet because no way those fat pricks would fit in an economy seat. Slimy Thailand sex-tourists. I feel like I need a shower – I'm grimy; uneasy. Larry says he needs a pint. Don't we all. Some gaff is serving Estrella in cardboard pint cups, out of a window like how you'd buy an ice-cream on the promenade on the English coast. As Larry queues up, a familiar face shouts my name, young Ed is bowling out of the supermarket towards me, his arms weighed down with carrier bags full of booze. I call out his full name and title; *Oi! Ed Sokolowski Mixing-Editing-Production!* He laughs, lifting his arms up to show me his treasure in the plastic bags – they're full of cartons of Sangria and he grins, *only one Euro a pop, Walts!* while beaming another wide smile. Ed tells me he'll be drinking and tanning himself on the beach, can't go wrong with the Sangria at that price, and then I remember something he tweeted about a while back about a beer festival in Finland when you float down the River in a boat, it struck me so I made a note in my memos on my phone, and seeing Ed now has reminded me of it.

I ask him to explain it to me – I tell him I've pictured myself floating down a River in a dinghy with a load of booze. He tells me that it's really popular now, about five thousand took part last year, it's called *Kaljakellunta,* which means simply 'beer floating' – you sit in an inflatable dinghy floating down a River and booze it up. Some people use self-built rafts. I tell him I'm gonna do this for my birthday one year, but Ed replies that the date is usually a secret until the last minute, probably a website you can check, or a newsletter you can subscribe to – be a bit difficult to get to Finland and to a location by a River at the drop of a hat – so I say maybe I'll start my own one, and Ed agrees and says he'd best get the booze to the lads on the beach, so we say bye. As I watch Ed walk down the street towards the beach, I'm reminded of Moon walking away from me in Valencia. I can't believe that was only yesterday. As if on cue, Ed turns his head to look over his shoulder and I wave at him, he lifts one of his plastic supermarket carrier bags up in acknowledgement, disappears into the crowd, and I light a cigarette to push away the pine for a Sangria.

Down at the square by Burger King, you can feel the heat from the sun on your neck and your head and your arms; I'm reflecting on the combination of scents; burgers and processed cheese, browning lettuce and cheap ketchup, tobacco smoke mixed with the welcome waft of more suncream on the breeze – plus the unmistakable smell of spilt lager on the floor, on shirts, on shorts, on jeans, in hair – slowly going stale and sticky as it dries in the sun. The singing of the hundreds of English lads before me, could be five-hundred, maybe more, fills the air, makes an atmosphere. Over-priced cardboard pints of flat Estrella are clutched all over, rubbish from Burger King litters the floor, hundreds of empty, crushed cups are strewn beneath a thousand pairs of trainers. Someone is pointing at a young black man crouched down, his short dreads bounce about as he grins in delight with perfect bright, white teeth, shouting *Come! Come!* He's wearing a Ghana kit – the material as white as his teeth – he turns to make an initial swift sale, others instantly follow. I can see ESSIEN printed boldly at the top – he stands to hand keen shoppers their product and I see BLACK STARS printed at the base of the kit – he's making a proper quick buck selling supermarket cans from his giant sports bag – he loves it – and now he sings along and nods in time as lads sing *Michael Essien* at him. Above my head a *Barca! Barca!* chant suddenly cuts through everything, gets everyone's attention in an instant. Up in the flats alongside one section of the square, a Catalonian can bear the Chelsea songs no more, he's safe up there, he's got a bright Barca away top on, a small Barca flag taut between his hands as he leans out of his window five floors up, crying out: *Barca! Barca!* His long bleached blonde hair is dancing in time as he shakes his flag and sings, then as the jeers die down and he takes a pause, the piss-taking begins: *Man or a woman? Are you a man or a woman? Maaaaan or a woman? Are you a man or a woman?* I watch him with intrigue. He has got no answer, up there with his bleached, long barnet, and then comes: *One Robbie Savage, there's only one Robbie Savage!* And everyone starts laughing, poor fella has got five hundred lads all laughing at him five floors below and he probably doesn't even know who Robbie Savage is. A lady appears next to him, maybe she's his partner, maybe a room-mate, who knows, she ain't stroppy but I can tell she's encouraging him to give it up before it gets nasty, *don't worry about it, come back in,* but he turns around and yells at everyone in his native tongue which prompts a few beer cups to get launched up at him, with a: *You what? You what? You what, you what, you what?* And then the icing on the cake, a tribute to the manager of Real Madrid, ex-Chelsea boss, they beat Barca at the weekend in their backyard so they are hurting big time – the hundreds chant a defiant: *José Mourinho! José Mourinho! José Mourinho, José Mourinho!* And as the beer cups reign up to him some more, he steps back and shuts his windows just as a half-filled supermarket can from Michael Essien's giant sports bag goes *thump* on the pane.

Larry is thirsty and I don't want to be on my own, so at the Hotel we grab our match-tickets and jackets, I secure a pin badge over my breast pocket, and then we're straight back out. I need to dig in really because I could put my head on the pillow right now. At the train station Larry buys two tickets, one each, he explains to me it's like a travel card, will be valid for the rest of the day, and then he pauses for a minute and changes his mind. He cocks his head to the side and says, *shall we walk?* and I reply, *sure,* and he says, *use these after the game,* and as he pockets the travelcards I still don't tell him how tired I feel, I'm tired in my legs, I'm tired in my head and I could easily sleep for three or four hours, and sleep just as long again and more in the evening, at my proper bedtime, but I get like this – I don't want to be on my own, and not wanting to be on my own overrides everything. *I don't want to be on my own.* Larry nips in a shop and comes out with a bottle of San Miguel, it's got a different label on than the usual, it's a stronger brew, Larry says it's proper cold, almost like it's been in the freezer, and I think of condensation running down a window in winter time as I watch the drips race around the label and down the side of his bottle.

It's still a few hours until kick-off, I'm laid up in the corner of a caff, cream Formica tables with salt and pepper pots, a silver box with small, square serviettes in, I've got a Coke and I've devoured an omelette, I had to sit down, I was proper drowsy. Larry promised me he'll be back in an hour, the lads from Putney have been on the phone and they're holed up in a gaff just up the road. I tell Larry to take his time if he wants and then I remembered I don't want to be on my own, but I can't stop him, I don't want to stop him, it's the semi-final of the second leg of the European Cup, I've got my corner, I'm settled physically but not settled mentally, so I start my breathing exercises, the scent of anti-bacterial spray is ripe. I begin this mild meditation because when Larry left, my anxiety started to fizz like the bubbles from the Coke jumping at the top of the glass, and as I move my head a little lower towards my knees I inwardly request for *El Espíritu Santo* to send a gentle wave of peace that only it can bring.

There's an empty table next to me and a lady sits down in the vacant seat. I didn't even see her come in. It was her sudden, deep sigh that alerted me to her presence. Her noise gently moved me out of my zone – no idea how long I've been slumped forward in my seat. As I study her, I get a lump in my throat – she is the spitting image of my Mum's big sister! It's mental when this happens, whenever I'm away somewhere there is always somebody who reminds me of someone I know – not just physically but also in the way they talk and as they gesticulate and as they unconsciously shift in their seat or sip their coffee, stuff like that. She stretches out her right leg, and that's when I notice her walking stick propped up next to her, and I instinctively say a reassuring *hi* without even thinking and she's a little startled. *Oh! You're English!* she states, just like Moon exclaimed yesterday. She looks pretty tired, all weary, like it's been a long day or a long week or a long month, it's sitting right there in her eyes as she takes off her glasses, removes a small, square serviette from the silver box on her table and that makes me think about Larry and Liz's situation and how he's not mentioned the IVF turmoil yet, but that's ok, he will when he's ready, if he wants to, without a prompt from me.

The Lady Who Looks Like My Aunty announces, *I've been to the British Consulate,* while adjusting her polished glasses on her nose. Her dark, bobbed hair has a little grey in it, the wrinkles in her face put her in her seventies, no doubt. I turn to my right, crossing my left leg over my right leg to face her and show her I'm listening. She puffs out her cheeks, laces her fingers together and rests her hands on the cream table. I suddenly feel fidgety for a cigarette, but I'm indoors, this time last year would've been different, but the smoking ban kicked in over here, in some ways I don't mind, it is what it is. I quickly glance around; I see a painting of a boat in a bay with cliffs to each side and yellow sand meeting the calm ocean. Another painting is of two couples dancing – him in a black suit and tie with a white shirt, her in a red dress that's hugging her figure, she's looking down at her raised heel, her left leg kicking up at an angle poised level at his waist, it nudges me back to Buenos Aires, I'm in awe as I study a couple performing the Tango, a dance originating down amongst the ports on the natural border of Argentina and Uruguay, beauty in poverty in motion. I turn away from the painting and nod with a smile at The Lady Who Looks Like My Aunty, giving her my full attention, it's one of those conversations where I might end up getting a bit of a life-story, but I don't need to make an excuse to leave because I realise I'm not shifting uneasily or uncomfortably in my seat, my breathing is normal, there's a gentleness in the voice of The Lady Who Looks Like My Aunty and I'm willing to listen intently:

To escape the British winters, I went to live in the South of France. I'd sold my Post Office in Tolladine, Worcester and bought three mobile homes! One to live in in France and two on a huge tourist campsite in Playa d'Aro near Girona (here in Spain!) to rent out to holiday-makers and hopefully bring in some cash. My homes were situated almost a mile from reception which was open every day. Well, last week I went into Playa and drew some cash from the bank and did some shopping and went back to camp. As I drove back, I noticed through the window my dog Rimu barking at something and that the door was open. I immediately turned around and flew back to reception to get the owner and I came back to my home which had been ransacked, every drawer opened, my bag with all my money, driving license and passport etc. gone. I had no means of identity and no way of getting any more cash from the local bank. After going to the police, the campsite owner allowed me to phone my brother David to transfer some money to a bank in Barcelona. So here I am. I've been to the bank, and I've been able to get a temporary passport from the British Consulate and I am able to fly back to UK on Thursday – in two days. There were no flights tomorrow!

I inform The Lady Who Looks Like My Aunty that five thousand Chelsea fans are over for a match tonight, so most of them will be on flights home tomorrow. I ask her what she's going to do next. She pauses while the waitress serves her food to her. She thanks the waitress, I motion towards her to eat if she wants, or to continue talking if she wants – or both. My seated companion sighs, puts fingers behind her glasses and rubs her eyes. I pick up my knife and fork and rearrange them on my plate, keeping my focus on her. She continues:

I think I might call it a day and move on. I've had a bit of a run of bad luck since I've been here, you see. A couple of years ago, I'll give you the short version, there was another English family settled at the mobile home park. The boyfriend of the English family's daughter had had a spare key cut, without them knowing, and got it later transpired that my car (a small Renault Five!) had been used to steal mobile homes including a large luxury Dutch mobile home off the site and over the border to goodness knows where! I was working in a bookshop you see, that I'd purchased from some friends I'd met. They had put the business up for sale to go and work at another resort somewhere. So, while I was working in the bookshop, my car was being used without me knowing! Then, last year, I managed to break both legs at the same time. It's quite easy to break both legs, just stumble in a hollow in a lawn! Friends took me to the hospital where I was plastered up and sent home. After six weeks I had no way of getting back to the hospital as the summer season was in full swing and my friends had their own businesses to look after and also I didn't have enough money to pay the hospital (one had to pay up front!) so I took a hammer and a chisel and cut down both sides of plaster, so I could clamp it back on if needs be. Anyway, I survived.

I looked at the walking stick by her side, and then she asked if I'd excuse her as she needed to visit the toilet. I looked at my empty plate. She picked up her stick and maneuvered gingerly around the table. I wondered who was looking after her dog, Rimu, while she was in Barcelona and then flying back to England. When the door of the toilet closed behind The Lady Who Looks Like My Aunty, Larry walked in with an alcohol glow plastered all over his smiling face. I stood up and walked to the counter, I paid for my food and also settled the bill for whatever The Lady Who Looks Like My Aunty had ordered. I hoped it would put some wind in her sails, bring some life to her bones, catapult some restoration into her soul, balance kindness from where she'd been robbed, a genuine gesture to fill her heart. As the owner turned to her till to put in the notes I gave her, I took a business card from the counter and shoved it in with the others in the back-right pocket of my jeans.

On another day I'd walk all around the ground, like I did on my last Euro away after flying into Athens with Den and Taxi Alan, what a spectacle, the Karaiskakis Stadium, in Piraeus, Attica, the home ground of Olympiacos. Attica always made me think of Atticus Finch in *To Kill a Mockingbird,* his daughter called Scout, I always like that name, don't know why, it's just one of those things. Outside Camp Nou, Larry takes a photo of me next to Hurry Up Dave who is clutching a plastic bag full of *cfcuk* fanzines, it makes me wonder how Ed with his plastic bags full of Sangria is getting on. I climb the stairs slowly. After the corrupt disgrace at Stamford Bridge against tonight's opposition, (Wednesday 06th May 2009), I vowed to never attend another European Cup fixture again. And I haven't. Until now. Maybe the demons will be exorcised. Who knows? I just had to get out of the house, you know? Larry has done me a right favour, he could have carried on boozing, but we're up here in the top tier of the Nou Camp, only a few hundred other fans dotted around coz it's early, and I lay out on the seats, looking up at the sky, it's colder now, I cross my arms over my chest and tuck my hands under my armpits, I've got no idea how high up I am, I hear Larry buying a drink off some fella going round with a plastic tub full of drinks, I feel like I'm floating, the sedatives in my system swimming round and massaging my temples and encouraging my eyes to close so I obey and I close them, five floors up in this shit hole, what will be will be, I wonder if everyone is safe from the Old Bill, it's a risk coming out here, someone somewhere will get caught out, it's the law of averages, we'll see how it pans out, as for the game well we're one nil up from the first leg, no doubt the officials will find a way for UEFA's favourite team to progress against who they believe are the enemies of football.

Straight from the kick-off, we're in down their left. Ashley Cole nipping in and playing the ball across. We are fucking buzzing up here, come on. Cahill is limping off with twelve minutes gone, twelve bloody minutes. The noise is incredible, over 95,000 in here apparently. A steward in front of me is removing a *CHELSEA NEW YORK* flag from the netting, and a man (who I got to know as Frank when I bumped into him down The Cock on North End Road over five years later) is pushing past me to go down the yellow steps to remonstrate with the steward, what the fuck is the steward doing, just leave the flag alone, no doubt deliberately provoking the supporters with his orange bib on, the flag causing no harm to anyone, Old Bill setting him up for it, maybe. I look down to the pitch to see Bosingwa jogging on to go right back for Cahill, Ivanovic moving next to John Terry at centre back, Frank from New York all red in the face coming back up the stairs after remonstrating with the stupid twat of a steward. Barca are slicing through us, we can't keep the ball, and there you have it, one nil to them, Busquets, the prick. Larry looks demoralised, the drink from the last couple of days taking its toll, all this time, all this money, all this build up, and it's falling apart again. We haven't had a chance to take it in or get our foot on the ball when some little Barca prick is rolling on the pitch, here we fucking go and you feel everything go out of us like a helium balloon deflating in sped-up-motion, the ref is giving a red card, it's John Terry, it's a fucking stitch up, Čech is in there consoling JT, ushering him off the pitch, I don't even know and can't even tell what's gone down out there – no-one can – but we don't need convincing it'll probably be as soft as melted ice-cream – we've just got to get to half-time, somehow. Someone says *Terry will be out for the final if we get there* well we ain't fucking getting there, are we, and still they come and still they exaggerate their falls and still they probe with their tippy-tappy bollocks, corrupt pricks, I'm trying to work out what the formation is, we're getting pulled all over the place, Bosingwa has slipped in next to Ivanovic and Ramires is right back, well he's supposed to be I think, but he's lost with another one of their quick one-twos and fucking hell it's two-nil. Plenty stream out. I see them to my right – I'm more over to the left of the away end – suddenly I feel cold – right before half-time and someone says *we could get proper turned over here* – everyone is thinking the same, ten men and two down already, then fuck me, hang on, is that Ramires up there? Is he through? He fucking is as well – he's scored *HE'S FUCKIN' CHIPPED HIM* – there's no flag, I'm looking for a flag, no flag, a bolt goes through my chest, we've fucking scored, *IT STANDS YYYYYYEEEEES YEEEEES YEEEEES YEEEEES FUCKIN YEEEEEES AWAY GOAL* – it's ages before I catch my breath, I need a piss, it's half-time, this is unbelievable – people are holding their heads and rubbing their eyes, we've got an away goal, ten men, I venture down the steps, there are fans on the concourse who don't believe we scored, they came down at two-nil and people are saying *Ramires, fucking Ramires,* and people are going *eh? You sure?* and they're jubilant: *He's chipped him! Rami's fuckin chipped him!* and people are going *nah, fuck off* – and others are going *it's 2-1 mate, we've scored* – I've never seen anything like it. I come out of the bogs and I hear screams of pain. There's a lad on the floor, mid-twenties, ginger hair and a Chelsea top on – he's screaming at three disinterested Old Bill towering over him – *Look what you done to my fuckin' leg LOOOK* – he's got tears in eyes, they're not bothered, they peer down dismissively at him, he carries on – *my ankle, you cunts, you fuckin cunts* – the sweat is pouring off him and I look down and his ankle is fucked, his foot is twisted round, all bent, they've dished it out with their batons so severely they've broken his fucking ankle, I walk on, I have to, his mates are with him, what am I supposed to do. I move up the stairs to find my way back to Larry and there is this bloke in front of a steward screaming blue murder at him: *You Catalan cunts mugged me, my wallet, my match-ticket – where's my money? Where's my seventy Euros? You owe me seventy Euros! You fuckin scumbags! Cunts!* Purple streaks of rage are splattered over his face like split beetroot on a chopping board. He's consumed by rage, I have to double-check, I wonder if I'm dreaming, he's not letting up, *I fuckin' hate you cunts,* it's both fascinating and worrying, I wonder where his mates are – they should be pulling him away in case it escalates, I need to clear my head. I go back to Larry and we walk just a few rows up and we are right at the back of the upper tier. There's no netting, nothing. I put my arms over the concrete and look down, five floors to the ground, what a way to go. We look out over the streets for a bit, then move back down, people coming back for the second half now. Looks like Mata, Lampard, Mikel and Meireles all in a line – Drogba dropping into left-back covering Ashley, this is ridiculous, backs against the walls, ten men, come on Chelsea. We're gonna defend it for forty-five minutes, and then out of nowhere I can see Drogba still there in the left-back position and something's happened, it's up the other end of the pitch, it's a fucking penalty. Heads are in hands all over the place, we haven't even played five minutes, the hope has been sucked back out as quickly as it had been injected in. The little twat Messi is up against Čech. Someone is yelling *Come on, Petr! Come on Petr! Come on, Petr!* It turns into a growl, animal like *COME ON PETR! COME ON PETR!* There's a girl leant into her boyfriend, her shoulders have sagged, she is devastated, desolate – people have got their hands over their faces, people have got their hoods pulled up and over their eyes, people have got their backs turned, people have got their hands in their pockets, people have got their hands folded across their chests, people have got their hands locked together placed behind their heads, people are looking at the floor, people are looking to the dark skies above, people are crossing their fingers, people are staring at the scene in front of them, people are craning people are praying – *THUNK* – he's missed *HE'S HIT THE FUCKIN' BAR HE'S HIT THE BAR HE'S HIT THE BAR HE'S HIT THE BAR HE'S-HIT-THE-BAR-HE'S-HIT-THE-BAR-HE'S-HIT-THE-BAR HAAAAAAAA AAAAAA* – no-one knows what the fuck is going on and you know the next thing that goes through your mind is if the ref is going to order a retake, like when everything stopped before Terry got sent off, then you are processing it in your mind, brain overloading, and Terry has gone, off – and here the whistle doesn't go, there's not gonna be a retake, the little prick has missed it, maybe Čech got a touch even, who knows. When Barca chances get cleared, I can see our players high-fiving each other, geeing each other up, you dare not entertain any hopeful thoughts, I can see Iniesta's goal beating Čech in the last minute back in 2009, I'm in the Harding Lower, Den next to me absolutely broken. I'm finding it hilarious that Bosingwa is at centre-back, Drogba now at right back – he has a pop from half-way but he doesn't get enough height on it – ten white Chelsea shirts behind the ball – Mata's legs are going – he's a lovely little player – Salamon Kalou comes on and Drogba has returned to the left again now as the minutes drag past – fuck me I feel exhausted – and someone says, *Torres is coming on,* and someone is yelling *TEN MINUTES, CHELSEA, TEN MORE FUCKIN' MINUTES* and I say to Larry: *I'm no statto or nothing, but I'm pretty sure Torres has got a decent record scoring here* and those minutes drag on, it is guaranteed that injury time will be extended far over what the allowance will be – what will happen is, is that there should be three minutes of time added on, but they'll show six, and the ref will play eight – I need a drink – still the seconds take longer to tick by than ever before – then sure enough, down that left side again BANG they score *FUCK* they've scored, but someone near me is screaming *OFFSIDE! OFFSIDE!* And I can see the flag up, he's fucking offside, this is unreal, I can't digest this shit, they come again and again, the ball pings OFF THE POST and Torres is over at left back now, mopping up, *COME ON CHELSEA,* bollocks to their onslaught – a ball comes over for Torres and we've got runners pegging it forward but he loses it, he fucking loses it, you berk, Fernando – *YOU ONLY HAD TO CONTROL IT, HOLD IT, SQUARE IT* and now there's ANOTHER free kick to them – this is getting stupid, two lines of white, *COME ON, CHELSEA* – a ball gets pinged in, the home crowd are SCREAMING for a hand-ball, BAYING for another penalty – but the ball is hoofed clear – hang on HANG ON my-left-palm-goes-out-onto-Larry's-chest-I've-got-a-fist-full-of-his-jacket and I look-at-the-lino-there's-no-flag-NO-FLAG – *Larry, he's onside* – TTT...*TTTORRES IS ONSIDE HE'S ALL ALONE GO ON GO GO GO GO ON* – he's-round-the-keeper *YES YES YES YES YES YES AAAAAAGGHHHHHHHHHHHH HE'S-SCORED-HE'S-SCORED-HE'S-SCORED* and Larry takes my wrist with his hand, I'm still clutching his jacket in my fist (much later he told me that I was pinching his skin) and I let go and I look to my right to witness an utter sea of madness; absolute euphoria it's an out-of-body experience sometimes there just aren't words – the whistle has gone, the whistle has gone, our players are back over – you just cannot believe it – got a lock-in now, maybe an hour – who gives a fuck – did all of that really happen – maybe twenty minutes later I find myself I looking to the back, only a few rows to the top of the tier, and there's a group of lads shoulder-to-shoulder all from the *Rivals* message board – Stan and Brad and Campo and then I realise it must be Famous that is with them – the fella with the beetroot cheeks that was going spare at the steward at half-time earlier.

I don't know how long we're held in but the next thing I know is that we're walking out of the ground, like a blue and white snake going down and round and round and down in a multi-storey carpark, there's a mixture of delight and unbelief and exhaustion and dehydration and elation and pure adrenalin – and we're a few of the first to walk into the Metro and Larry finds the right line at Collblanc station, but both our travel cards are rejected. They re-appear out of the slot and the barriers remain stubbornly shut. At the next ticket machine, a lad just jumps over it because his card has been rejected too. I follow suit, jumping over, then Larry behind me. Everyone starts doing the same, more Chelsea boys are piling into the station. I look behind me to the left and then to the right, there's no staff in sight, one sleight lad lies on his front and shuffles his body under the barrier, there's enough space for him to fit. As we walk in the direction of the platform we need, I turn around and watch everyone piling over the line of ticket machine barriers, reminds me of Baker Street tube before a Cup semi at Wembley before we played Luton Town – as Larry and I turn the corner down on to the platform we can hear the subway train approaching and then a sound of breaking glass accompanying the unmistakable English roar as Chelsea kick-in the barriers, breaking them down, concentrated commotion more than a confused melee; essential, focused vandalism to provide the clear exit for everyone to step through rather than climb over, we get on the subway train with thirty or forty others as an emergency alarm rings out above us, it's all kicked off.

There's a bloke I know from the Harding Lower in our carriage, I don't know his name, just another one of those where you've always been on nodding terms. He's sunburnt and he's bewildered, and for a couple of stops he just repeats over and over: *Nou Camp, ten men, Messi missed penalty TEN MEN, Bosingwa centre-back, Drogba left-back, Messi missed penalty, ten men! TEN MEN!* He's in shock. Before we jump off at Sants Estació, Larry takes a photo of us.

The thing is with mental ill-health is that you can't really articulate the what and why sometimes, but it is what it is, and what happened next was, Larry and I returned to the Hotel, I went to bed, and he went back out. (It was days later that I guessed that no-one's travel cards worked because if it was past midnight, they had expired.) Lying on my bed in my boxer shorts, my adrenalin was high. I'd taken my sedative, but I was stunned processing what I'd witnessed. For some reason, I put the television on – it was tuned to Barca TV and a re-run of the match had just started – the players were jogging out! Extended highlights! You couldn't make it up. I sat on the edge of my bed watching it all over again, electricity coursing through me – and after Torres scores Bobby Di Matteo and Eddie Newton are dancing and hugging and spinning and right then I told myself that it doesn't matter what happens in Munich because what I have just witnessed is the most incredible, extraordinary, bonkers football match I have ever seen, or ever likely to see, ever again, and as my eyes finally closed as drowsiness overtook adrenalin, I could see Di Matteo and Newton hugging and spinning – almost twirling – and it struck me that it was just like a couple at the train station yesterday when the fella holding a red rose by the escalator took his partner in his arms and kissed and twirled her around – and also just like in my dream last night, Carla and Jo twirling and spinning and hugging. Bobby and Eddie. What a pair. Little old Chelsea, eh? We're going to Munich. My brain shut down with a twirl and a spin, there were no visions, only a peace that surpassed understanding.

Chapter Six

HOME

Wednesday 25th April 2012

It was landing in Buenos Aires eleven years ago that I first experienced an aeroplane full of passengers applauding a successful descent. I joined in with gusto – more of a release than anything else, that I was safe on solid ground. Now as the plane's tyres kissed the Gatwick tarmac, I couldn't resist starting the applause for a bit of a giggle more than anything else, Larry shot me a laugh through the cloud of his hangover and together we sang *Chelsea! Chelsea! Chelsea!* Brad and Stan, who had taken the same route as us with a train to Valencia airport, shook their heads, continuing to look worse for wear after pulling an all-nighter in La Rambla after last night's miracle. Fixture congestion is a massive issue for the loyal supporters. Yesterday was Chelsea's tenth game in thirty-two days, probably why loyalty points for last night's match went down to zero, especially because there's an FA Cup Final to pay for on the fifth of May, and those tickets don't come cheap. The team have played Benfica (home and away), Barca (home and away), Spurs and Wigan at home in the league, Spurs in the FA Cup semi plus away games at Villa, Arsenal and Fulham. A game every three days. I had a ticket for Arsenal, but I couldn't get out of bed. I struggled to get to the toilet because of giddiness and that – let alone travelling to North London. The only match I went to out of this batch of fixtures was the game at Craven Cottage on the ninth of April. It took me over an hour to shuffle my way, (with Larry and Champagne Les), from the Eight Bells to the ground. Super Frank scored a penalty; Clint Dempsey equalised. I was lucky not to burn my house down on a couple of occasions. I left some Oxtail Soup simmering and fell asleep on the sofa, no idea for how long. When I awoke, the soup had all burnt out, a brownie-black tar remained like the excavated lung of a heavy smoker. I turned off the gas, gripped the handle to move the saucepan, and burnt my hand. A similar thing happened a few days later, this time with frozen peas, I'd forgotten to put any water in the saucepan. I got lucky with the kids, too. After zoning out and falling asleep, they had positioned a large mirror (that Josie used as she rehearsed dance routines) against the sofa, and were sliding down it. The glass shattered. I awoke to my daughter by my side softly calling my name, telling me there'd been an accident. I went downstairs to find my son sitting and playing amongst shards of jagged mirror glass, the film they'd had on the TV long finished. I was all over the place.

There's something reassuring about only having hand luggage, skipping baggage collection with nothing to stand about for and nothing to declare, leaving the conveyor belt behind us as it continues bumping round and round waiting for cases to drop in, most of the passengers stand fidgety and impatient, whereas Larry and I go directly to passport control. We go our separate ways with a heart-felt hug, he saunters off to his platform to go to Putney via Clapham, I make my way to platform two; rucksack secure over both shoulders. I stand with my arms folded looking around, plenty of time to kill until my train pulls up, I'm in no rush, I'm in one of those moods where I wouldn't even care if there were delays. I instinctively pat down my pockets, makes a change to a steward outside an away end doing it for me. It feels like something is missing, my phone usually resides in my front right pocket, oh *of course,* it's in my rucksack, maybe it feels like something is missing because I need to turn my mobile on, my brain telling me that something is out of place, the pattern of addiction well established; home button; swipe to unlock; check messages and notifications. No wonder our spirits crave for solitude and solace – the only time we experience absolute quiet is during a respectful minute's silence. Mobile phone addiction is similar to the craving for a cigarette once your first pint is two-thirds in, or when I'll eventually step off this train and can light up, or the rush of water from the tap in the morning to fill up the kettle and your brain knows nicotine is imminent. I could well do with a cup of tea now – can't remember when I last had one – but for now my phone needs my attention like a long-forgotten pot-plant on the windowsill thirsting for a watering. I pull the blasted thing out of the front pocket of my rucksack and turn it on, irritated now. I keep it in my palm but I refold my arms, the handset gripped in my right palm, my right palm nestling under my left armpit. I think back and work out that it's been turned off since Larry reappeared in Valencia after I spoke to my Mum, just before I chatted to Moon. Seems weeks longer than the forty-eight hours that it actually is.

A plane roars overhead under cumulous clouds, the whining, creaking machine climbing slowly up, a wonder of gravity and science, the noise overbearing like the squealing of a coffee machine and the banging of the metal cylinder holding the used granules, the dark brown grains squashed and refusing to budge until the girl with a branded apron bangs the handle more firmly. Studying the underbelly of the plane, I imagine bolts bending and nuts snapping, metal scraping and wings wobbling – I shiver with a flash of anxiety, I can't swallow, worry is pouring into my body from my brain, like milk splashing and mixing into a tall glass of coffee, my feet feel like they might lose their grip on the concrete, dampness invades the material under my armpits – I wheel around and identify an empty metal bench screwed down, I walk over to it – mercifully there's no-one sitting on it – I purposefully take a deep breath and hold it down in my lungs as I sit, I slowly count to six, it occurs to me that the air in my lungs is polluted – trains and cars and planes, exhausts and contrails and fumes. I start gulping air down like a hungry, crying baby trying to attach on a nipple, the baby needs soothing, they're dependent on it – I try and block out of my head that the air I'm gulping is full of filth and dirt – I tell myself I'm on solid ground, that I have space to breathe, that I am fearfully and wonderfully made, that I'm going home, that I can lean back in Jah's love, a love that's like no other and I don't need to get up for work, I made it through the flight, I can sleep all day when I get home. A recorded announcement makes me jump as it blares out that in a few minutes my train will be approaching, the same voice in the same tone reads out all the calling points. I close my eyes and repeat my breathing exercises and quietly repeat the calling points in unison with the announcement. I remind myself that there are no rules, I can step off the train whenever I need to at whatever stop I choose. There, I can gather my thoughts, steady my being, wait for my head to be in a place that is ready for me to board the next train going my way and try again. There are no rules. There is no rush. I've got nowhere to be, I've got no deadline to meet, I've got no multitude of stairs to climb because I can't face the lift, no compact office to feel squashed in, no opportunity for the prickles of claustrophobia to start stabbing, and if they do I can simply get off the train and sit on a bland, metal bench all screwed down, just like this one but at a different station further southwest, and if the bench is full I can leave the station and walk around the block, maybe wait for the 700 bus that serves the whole coast from Brighton to

Portsmouth, (there's a bus stop at the top of my road), or maybe I'll lie down towards the end of the platform, empty of other passengers, use my rucksack as a pillow, put my headphones in, listen to a meditation, read a Psalm, make a phone call, Jah's love will sustain me, fall asleep with my knees pulled up to my chest, there are no rules, there is no rush, and now my palm is vibrating, vibrating, vibrating.

I assume it's a call coming in, but when I turn my palm towards my face and have a look, it's text after text after text dropping in. I watch the screen with a smile, feeling each accompanying vibration on my skin as the text count rises. Sandwiched between one from Josie asking if I have landed okay, (the most recent), and one from my Mum before I powered down and turned off the handset in the old town of Valencia, (the oldest unread one), my inbox is bursting with congratulations aplenty from pals old and new, far and wide and even a couple of numbers where the contact isn't saved – no idea who they are. I have texts from fans of Southampton (Blanco, Nick), West Ham (Nev, Royal Paul, Lucky Zack), Blackburn (Jossie's Gaints), Arsenal (Zammo), Everton (Toffee Colin, Jeff), Fulham, (Pete, Wozza), Watford (Ian), Liverpool (Dan, Azza, Darren), Brighton (Seagull Si), Halifax Town (Jonny Angel) and message after message from Chelsea pals who had watched the match in pubs wishing they were in our end with Larry and I. I slowly read them all, smiling at every text, I dutifully reply to each of them, purposefully leaving my reply to Zammo the Gooner until last. I ask him: *No mate, I have no idea what you're on about!* ☺ *What is a Gary Neville scoregasm, please?* – I was so wrapped up in these replies I didn't notice my anxiety evaporating into the atmosphere to silently disperse into the aeroplane vapour trails above me.

As the train approaches, I put my phone on mute. I stand and move towards the side of the train door and wait for three people to disembark, two of them dragging huge dark suitcases, I wonder if they're catching a flight home or leaving England to travel on holiday. I reach out and grasp the small black handle to steady myself and step up carefully on to the carriage, the noise of their whining suitcase wheels being dragged across the platform join in unison with plenty of others as eight carriages full of travellers pulling cases with rattling wheels alight for the airport. They sound like an army marching for Queen and Country moving forcefully towards their destination, boots crunching on concrete in time. I punch the close button and watch the train doors shut together; the sound of restless suitcase wheels wrestling for space now muted like my mobile. Thankfully, passengers on the carriage are sparse. It's not that busy, I didn't think it would be, it's not half-term or anything, I can sit where I like, I take my usual spot – a seat by the window of a two-seater, no chance of anyone sitting next to me with a train this empty, no-one sitting in front, just the view to keep me company; I place my rucksack on the seat to my right. This is a train that left Portsmouth Harbour early doors, gone all the way up to London Vic via East Croydon and Clapham Junction – hundreds of commuters stepping off at their London destinations – brollies and polished shoes, ironed shirts under loud blazers holding bold ties, high heels and black tights under skirts or suits, builders and painters and decorators with dusty concrete on steel toe-capped boots or worn Reebok trainers, bright orange florescent bibs, flecks of paint and smears of dry concrete are decorating chequered jackets, hard-hats are cushioned in hands, breast pockets of shirts are cradling packets of tobacco with Rizlas and filters sealed expertly inside – the train sits at London Vic for a bit, the driver and conductor change, the carriages groan their way out of Victoria then pick up pace to go hurtling out of London towards Gatwick Airport where I step on. As the conductor rings the bells, I have a sudden thought that forces me back up and out of my seat. I walk up the carriage and sure enough, there it is, a well-read copy of this morning's newspaper discarded on a white table, folded in two. I flip it over to the sports page, there's a large photo of Fernando Torres on his knees with Ramires on his knees next to him with Frank Lampard on one knee in front of him and Frank is looking, he's looking up, looking up in wonder, a full grin laced with adrenaline and joy covers his face, and you know who he is looking up at, he's looking at the top tier, five thousand Chelsea going fucking bananas, we've beaten UEFA's love-hearts, the match-fixers will have to swallow this down, hope it sticks in their throats, we're going to Munich; ten men, Messi missed penalty, Bosingwa at centre back – my eyes have filled up with water, I shake my head and take the paper back to my seat and my solitude, thinking of Frank just looking up.

I pull down the plastic tray-table quickly and place the folded newspaper on it. When the table comes down to a secure position, it always produces an ear-splitting-God-awful screech, reminds me every time of fingernails down a blackboard, like Quint in the film *Jaws* when he sits in the corner of the Town Hall. He's drawn a Great White in chalk, mouth open, a chalk-stick-man between the shark's teeth, his fingernails slowly scraping down the blackboard getting everyone's attention. He tells the gathered Amity Island business owners and town councillors that he'll get the killer shark: *"I'll catch this bird for you, but it ain't gonna be easy. Bad fish."* It was because of that film that I read all about the *USS Indianapolis* – there's that scene on the boat when Hooper says to Quint: *"You were on the Indianapolis?"* and even though I was ignorant to what that meant at that time, a chill rushed through me. Through my twenties, I slowly purchased all the books by Peter Benchley, (except *Time and a Ticket,* it's out of print and over a hundred notes to buy online) – that's the thing, it's all about TIME, isn't it? And the money. Time and a ticket. If I had the time, and the money, I'd go all over. Not just the football, but hiking – the Camino Trail, the Royal Military Canal, the whole Welsh coastal path, the entire length of the Danube as it flows magnificently through ten countries and four national capital cities – the opportunities to walk are endless.

The rocking carriages soothe me. It's not always been like that. I close my eyes and go over memories of yesterday. I can smell the salt from the harbour as bottles of Estrella clink together; I can see my arm gripping Larry's chest as our end momentarily holds its breath as Torres bursts clear; I can hear the station getting smashed up above me as the Metro underground train pulls in, braking to a halt. I look out of my window, the train near Shoreham-by-Sea now. I can tell it's been raining all night, when the doors opened at the last station, (Southwick), I could smell the change in the air as I studied the still puddles on the platform, the wind had probably blown away the dark clouds by dawn, the sun getting stronger now in the late-April morning. As the train curves around a long corner, I can see a hot air balloon in the distance, above the South Downs, I guestimate it's flying near West Chilington where Amberley kisses Storrington on one cheek and Arundel on the other. The balloon is coloured red, yellow, blue, white and green – like a funny shaped beach ball – I wonder how many people are in the basket. It's a question I asked myself as a kid in the car with my big sister; Dad indicating left to pull off the A3, travel a few minutes and we'd get to Cherry Tree Road, I'd count the cherry trees and then we'd turn right at the roundabout, second exit, my anticipation would grow, inside I would eagerly hope that I'd see a hot air balloon – whoever caught a partial view first would announce it to the others, then came the joy and frustration of tracking it between trees and road as our car drove on. I'd always wonder how many people were riding in the wicker. Our blue Cortina estate would be making its way through the villages of Witley, Chiddingfold and Northchapel – I'd always read the signs displaying the name of the villages we'd pass through. If I was teased with a glimpse of a colourful balloon way up in the blue, it would fuel my desire to see more. I would crane my neck concentrating on the gap between the basket and the balloon, all I wanted was to set my eyes on was the fire; hoping to see the blast of yellow flame, swear sometimes I could hear the rush of gas. I'd be fascinated at the invisible hot air filling the balloon, wondering how and why the fabric never caught alight, even though I knew I would never be a passenger in one, I'd never experience the thrill and exhilaration of being up that high. I didn't care though, I couldn't fathom how you could be relaxed in that basket so high up, at the mercy of the wind and the flame, maybe my hair and then my clothes would accidentally catch on fire, I'd jump out, go down in flames, rich green of both tree and fields blurring with blue of sky and white of clouds as I tumbled to earth; the sharp, bitter twist in my nostrils of burning follicles followed by the taste of singed hair on my tongue, the pain of my burning flesh; and far down below on the A283, there is some kid looking out the back seat window of his Dad's motor, he is watching open-mouthed at a dropping, twisting body dancing in yellow and orange flames until it disappears between trees, he imagines the sickening thud of body on earth, he tries to alert his Dad but no sound comes, his mouth agape in bewildered fear, seconds later he wondered if he saw anything at all as the car quickly turns right, a big enough gap for his Dad to accelerate into, the vehicle turns off the A283 and on to a remote country lane, lurching towards Lurgashall.

I pull my phone out of my pocket to take my mind off falling to my death out of a hot air balloon. There's another text from Zammo, it simply reads 'scoregasm' with a YouTube link. I had no idea what to expect. I click the link and then a rush of euphoria floods me again; football – a drug like no other – Alan Parry's commentary complemented by Gary Neville's 'scoregasm' as Torres rounds Valdes, and I'm laughing and then the camera pans to Eddie and Robbie hugging and jumping, my eyes well up again, goose bumps smother my flesh, I find myself not caring what happens in Munich – we'll be up against either Bayern in their own backyard or José's Real Madrid, I will always have this moment, if I never went to a game again, I will always have this experience – I forward the 'scoregasm'

YouTube link to Larry, then I watch it again and again and again, Torres the wally trying to dribble it out and five seconds later he's clean through, I just can't get over it, and there is Frank, just looking up at us....

It's not an option to get a cab because I need to take my time, gather my thoughts, get my head straight. It's over a mile to walk home, and I'm happy to do it. I start to fill with mild dread about what might await me at home, maybe Josie has taken the kids to her parents again to escape the dark clouds of my depression, maybe as my kids embrace their loving Father, Josie will turn coldly away, arms folded frostily, hoping I don't start talking bollocks like instructing her to go and find someone else who will care for her better than I can. As I step off the train the air is immediately different to Gatwick – cleaner – the scent of purity, the smell of the long-gone downpour still hangs in the air, clinging on to the morning before the sun's peeking fully breaks through the clouds. I follow the road past the small row of shops, the 700 bus creaking around the mini roundabout, people on the top deck looking down on to the pot-plants decorating the bus shelters that have loved the over-night shower giving them sustenance and the ability to continue vividly blooming. It seemed to me that the clouds had travelled the same route as the train tracks, sandwiched between the South Downs way to their right, and the beach and ocean to their left, it unleashed torrents at first light – one of those downfalls where water smashes the ground like bullets against the floor. Puddles had grown bigger and bigger – ultimately connecting with each other – making one giant puddle that covered the pavements, spilling into the roads and rushing down the tarmac and paving where I currently tread. Now, with the sun pushing out, water begins to disperse, the breeze from the sea significant but not uncomfortably nippy. All along this section of the coast this morning, freshly laundered washing was hung on lines; as clothes pegs held garments, the hangers whispered to themselves that it was going to be a good drying day. I'd have a few loads of laundry to do once I got home. Josie never does this, it's my job, I do all the laundry – I insist. It's partly because I always have done it, was a good nine years between me leaving home and living with Josie, so it's simply carried on from there.

I flick my cigarette into the gutter as I turn into my road not knowing what to expect when I get home. I need a shower; I feel all sticky and unkempt. Leaning my head down towards my arm, I could smell my sweat. A few weeks ago, when I was last at the Doctor's, I spoke about some after-effects of my medication, explaining I would sweat profusely as soon as anxieties rose – I'd been using both roll-on and spray deodorant to try to stem the sweats. It wasn't working and I'd thrown out a few shirts – even when smothered with Vanish and on a high degree wash, dirty yellow stains and slight odour remained on material that had caught too many drips of pure anxiety from my arm pits. The Doctor suggested shaving the hair off. He explained how I'd then be using roll-on directly on to my pores, rather than coating hair first. I followed his advice. It's definitely made a difference. He suggested my rekindled and growing cigarette habit was the least of my worries – the priority was to rest, he reminded me I was physically and mentally exhausted and burnt out, having some stability was key. *Be still and know that I am Jah.*

Josie and I are renting a place that is a five-minute walk from the beach – the front garden sweeps in front of the house and round down the side of it. The washing line is attached to a black painted metal drainpipe at one end, and stretches all along to the shed at the other end. I can fit two loads of clean laundry on there. I step through the open gate and see a double bed sheet, a double duvet cover and four pillow cases hung on the washing line, flapping slightly in the breeze. I stop in my tracks and watch the washing for a bit, I know instantly that it's Josie's way of showing her love and devotion to me. One less job I have to do, (I don't mind doing it, in fact – it gives me a sense of role in the family unit, something I can tell the lads down the pub; *I sort out all the laundry – Josie hangs it all wrong.* Josie can take pride in it too, when explaining to the girls; *Oh, he sorts all that out. It's what he's always done. He doesn't let me touch it, tells me that I hang it wrong!*)

I put my key in the front door and push my way into silence. Josie is at work. I shower and go to bed, setting my alarm and then another alarm three minutes later in case I slept through the first. Sure enough, the second alarm saved me. I walk into town, collect my son from nursery, I carry him for a mile on my shoulders until we reach my daughter's school where I lift him off me and he runs to play on the slide. I wait away from the queue in the playground as the children in Reception file out. The class teacher and her assistant kneel with each child until they are united with a parent or a carer, I wait until last. I wave at my daughter's teacher who smiles and points my little girl in my direction. She runs up to me and I scoop her up in my arms, she tells me she missed me and I said I missed her too. She laughs while she says into my ear: *Mum said Chelsea won!* And rather than explain that it was a draw on the night but Chelsea still went through the final 3-2 on aggregate, it was easier to say: *Yes, honey. Yes, they did.* As we hug I pray that my dark clouds will disperse, I don't want to be ill, I long to work, I pine to get better, and in the arms of my daughter while I watched my son climbing up the steps to go back down the slide, I had everything I needed in this moment, and more.

After dinner I bathed the kids and put them to bed – my daughter in the top bunk and my son in the bottom. As Josie read them a bedtime story, I returned to the kitchen to load the dishwasher. I don't know long I'd been staring blankly out the window. Josie touches me on the shoulder to bring me back to myself, I watch her pour a glass of red wine and she asks me about my trip. We sit at the kitchen table, I tell her about The Lady Who Looks Like My Aunty, Josie spins her phone in her palm and googles Playa d'Aro, has a look at the campsite and flicks through some images and smiles; *Maybe we'll go camping there this summer?* I look Josie in the eye and tell her; *I've got a feeling I'm gonna get given a spare ticket for the Final* and she cocks her head to one side, asking *You going, then?* And I nod firmly and write a memo on my phone to prove it after it happens:

25/04/2012 WILL GET GIVEN A TICKET FOR THE EUROPEAN CUP FINAL

Later that night, Josie hooked one leg over mine and snuggled into me. As her hair tickled my nose, she rested her hand on my chest. I turned my face and smelt the faint fragrance of the fresh flowers she'd put on my bedside table. I felt her head rise to look up me, so I turned back towards her, she rose slightly more until her mouth, ever so softly, met mine. I could taste salt on her lips, I could smell the sea-breeze-dried bed sheets under my body, the pillow cases under my head and the duvet over us. The smell was healing. Her taste restoring. For the first time in months, our bodies fitted together like a completed jigsaw with gentle love for each other. Afterwards, I continued to hold her as she slept, her leg still hooked over mine. Her head rested on my chest; her arm draped over my stomach. I whispered *I love you* into her skin and silently cried.

PART TWO

"Drogba now. Having headed the equaliser close to the end of the normal ninety minutes can score, can win the Champions League on what will surely be his last performance for Chelsea. He's just a couple of yards of run-up. Neuer bouncing on his line. Drogba to win it. COME ON, DIDIER!"

Alan Green, commentator, Allianz Arena, Saturday 19th May 2012.

Chapter Seven

THE PRINCE OF WALES, 12 LILLIE ROAD, SW6 1TT

Friday 18th May 2012

We are sitting opposite each other at a table outside on the patio, the traffic on Lillie Road passing in front of us. Tall Paul smiles at me while I light a cigarette; he's shaking his freshly shaved head in disbelief; laughing into the froth of his lager saying it was less than three hours to fly from Gatwick to Stockholm in '98, this coach we're getting on shortly is going to take at least twelve hours to get to Munich. He sinks some of his pint and looks up to the sky, lock his hands behind his head and says: *The email says we've got one hour after the final whistle to return to the coach to go home. No exceptions. No waiting around. Then another twelve hours on the road. Minimum.* I poke at the slice of lemon in my Coke with the tip of my finger, swirl it around the ice, I scan panoramically from left to right at the hundreds of Chelsea fans gathered down Lillie Road, loads of them all getting on the piss – the starter before the main course, (power drinking on the ferry), the main course before dessert, (sneaky duty-free cans on the coach) then dozing until Munich. The beer garden out the front here is full, the paved area outside the Wee Imp is full, the space outside the Lillie Langtry just down the road opposite is full; I imagine if I were to stroll down Seagrave Road past the Atlas, their beer garden would also be full. With the fans drinking, it's no different to a pre-match early doors – like when it's a 3.00pm kick-off and you're in the pub around eleven in the morning, except the domestic season is over, everyone here is about to travel through the night to go to the European Cup Final.

Flags are draped all over the fencing, the bubble of anticipation in conversations dips and rises. A bewildered barmaid walks around the tables with two plates of fish, chips and peas looking for who ordered the food, all the staff stunned that the pub is so busy. Tall Paul nods towards her and says to me: *Rushed off their feet. Geezer at the bar reckons there's fifty coaches going.* I booked three 'platinum' seats with a company called 'Coach Innovations' early doors – I was straight in there as soon as they were advertised. One ticket for me, one for Tall Paul and one for George, they were the most expensive seats, I didn't want to be stranded on an old rust-bucket on the outskirts of Frankfurt with three hours until kick-off. Larry couldn't justify the trip for all kinds of reasons, we understood, (like when Tall Paul and I had to swerve Moscow in 2008), tomorrow night Larry will be watching the game at the next best place – just around the corner from here in one of the pubs down the Fulham Road. I knew it wasn't an option to fly to Munich, the cost and the ball-ache would have been huge. There were other ways around it, of course, flying to alternative airports and getting trains in. But, for me, it was simpler this way, sleep on a coach, see the match, sleep on a coach again. Tall Paul and I went with the official club trip to Stockholm for the Cup Winners' Cup Final in 1998 with Den and Jervo. It was about £300, none of us trusted old Ken Bates, so this was the only way we could guarantee flights and match-tickets together and Den especially didn't want to take the risk of missing out. I know plenty who wouldn't normally travel on the Club's official package, who have made an exception for this match. You can't blame them. It's the European Cup Final.

These 'platinum' coach tickets of ours meant two things – firstly, our seats reclined, and secondly, a host service was available to us. Tall Paul burst out laughing when he first read the email: *Platinum GUARANTEES a reclining seat!* During certain parts of the twelve-hour drive (minimum), one could order drinks and food – by food they meant a choice of three varying flavours of Pot Noodle. I wasn't knocking it; I was in instant-snack heaven with the choice of Chicken and Mushroom, Beef and Tomato or Chicken Chow Mein flavours. At least everyone on my coach would be well fed and watered and manage some kip. It wasn't until the week after Munich that I realised how lucky we'd been. Not only was our coach brand spanking new, it was the first out of the carpark to roar towards Dover, (we picked up George at the services in Maidstone along with a couple of other fans), it was one of only a few new coaches with the reclining seats and a host service. The coaches were all lined up in the huge carpark on Seagrave Road. In a few years, work would start on new flats on the site, and the carpark would be long gone. (A few seasons later when the building work was complete, on each occasion I walked to the Bridge I would take my time passing the Atlas pub, studying their colourful hanging baskets of flowers, look up at the bricks and mortar of the new builds – four-hundred grand for a one-bedroom flat – and reflect back on the photograph in my memory of fifty or more coaches lined up on the tarmac ready to drive to Munich.) The coach company were clear that consuming your own pre-purchased alcohol was not permitted while on the coach, and like everyone else I just thought good luck in enforcing that one, it's impossible. You just had to hope you didn't have too many selfish dickheads on your coach, good luck with that one, too, nothing worse than a wasted *Carefreeeeee* at 2.00am when you've only just nodded off, the stale, sweaty odour of fifty or so men still rising and wafting about under the dial for the insufficient air-con, a bag of Columbian being unwrapped down the back, someone puking loudly in the only toilet that's had twenty or thirty bowels unleash their waste to splash in the now filthy bowl. I had Imodium. Tall Paul puffs his cheeks out and stretches his arms above his head, he shakes his freshly shaved head in disbelief at me again, he laughs up to the heavens, locks his hands once more behind his head and repeats: *Watch the game, one hour from the final whistle to get back to the coach, another twelve hours. Minimum.* I tell him it's a good opportunity to catch up on some sleep, his three kids are at home with his missus, she told me she couldn't wait to get rid of him for the weekend – besides, it's the only way we can get to Munich now, and I probably wouldn't be able to dig deep enough to go on this coach without the security of strong mates; I'm still that fragile, I still go missing, I still need company with people I trust – *I don't want to be alone* – I'm still alcohol-free, still on the strongest sleeping pills that the Doctor can prescribe, two days ago I sat in his surgery and he said to me in a gentle, patient tone: *Take your time.*

It was in that moment I knew I had to accept my recovery was going to be longer than a few weeks or even months. Before my name was called, I sat in the corner of the waiting room with my hood up. I'd worked for ten years in the community, and I didn't want to see anyone I knew from the estate. I was filled with anger because I couldn't work, I was full of shame because the charity I ran was folding – and all because I was burnt out. Like the reaction of a child up at a urinal when an adult appears, I shy away slightly to the wall when I see Debbie walk through the door and up to the reception desk. She is one of the estate mums, she's got three sons; ten years I've known her. When the school referred her eldest son to my charity, he was ten years old. A decade on, and he's in prison. I pinched my hood at my neck and held my hand there, the muscles in my neck tightening and my stomach turning as I pushed down a dry retch to stop my breakfast rising up; *fuck, what's happening to me?* I'm in bad place here.

Debbie drops down in a plastic chair opposite me, its feet screwed to the floor to stop smack-heads picking them up and hurling them at the receptionists. I risk a glance out of the corner of my eye, she's concentrating on her phone screen, oblivious to me, poor old Debbie and her three boys. I remember her distraught face when her eldest son was first sentenced to Young Offenders after six years or more of anti-social behaviour. She knew he'd be in and out of the prison system for years now that he'd run out of chances. I remember her middle son's frustration in not understanding what was happening to his brother that caused his Mum such distress. He was unable to communicate verbally, and walked with a slight hunch – many mused that this was the result of the beatings Debbie took when he was in the womb from her violent partner, the spine never straightening as her second son grew, his tongue never untying as he developed. As things fell apart at home, the younger brother walked out of his classroom one afternoon and shimmied up on to the roof. He refused to come down, threatening to jump. I didn't try and coax him down like the others, (not that they were doing the wrong thing), I simply walked around the playground to another part of the school building, climbed up on to the roof at the other end, slowly walked towards him and saw he was lying down on his back, staring up at the sky. I lay next to him until he was ready to retreat down the ladder that the Premises Officer had secured in place. Social Services stepped in because the younger brother was now at a higher risk. He finally met the threshold of need after years of us and the school saying he was at risk – not the Social's fault – they're understaffed and underfunded with unsurmountable caseloads as the walls of a decent society crumble around us all like a mudslide crashing devastatingly down a mountain.

When the side-door opens and the Doctor appears and calls my name, I wince and steady myself. I was hoping he'd glance over and recognise me so that I could just get up and walk through the side-door. However, my fears were realised when, at the sound of my name, Debbie looks up from her phone and her eyes meet mine. I see her mouth open, I know my cheeks are gaunt and I've dropped a couple of inches from my waist; she smiles awkwardly and says to me: *Oi, where the fuck is my food hamper at?* And it isn't until months later when I was reflecting on it that I fully realise she was saying this in jest, in warmth, in love even – it was her way of expressing concern, everyone knew the project was closing and I was ill, estate gossip is like that, and she couldn't nurse me or pull my hood off my head and hug me like she would one of her sons, she went to her point of reference which is the hamper deliveries we'd sort at Christmas and at Easter for the families I knew that proper needed it, (or intermittently throughout the year when the situation demanded it), and she hadn't had a hamper for months. I'd have all these financial donations from churches in the area, one church leader said to me: *My car is broken, I go to the mechanic, he's got the tools. A family needs feeding, I give you the donation, you're on their doorstep, you've got their trust.* But when Debbie said: *Oi, where the fuck is my food hamper at?* I mumbled a *sorry* to her and shuffled out of the waiting room, tears filling my eyes, I leant my shoulder against the wall for balance, I wanted the surgery to open up and swallow me whole, I knew her eldest boy was in jail, her middle son in his late teens still non-verbally-communicative and possibly always would be, her youngest boy now running feral around the estate and beyond, fully excluded from the two Secondary schools that gave him chance after chance – and of course I blamed myself. However, this was just one family, the team I ran had eighty families on the caseload and I was guiltily turning down fresh referrals at least twice a week. The guilt gnawed at me like a giant rat ravenously chewing through wood to get to the sleeping chickens inside the safety of their coop. I felt a fake and a fraud, an insomniac who was too proud for the benefits I was entitled to for being signed off work, I lived in denial genuinely thinking I'd feel fine in the morning. That was about to change. The Doctor did an about-turn in his surgery doorway, saw me steadying myself against the wall trying unsuccessfully to follow him into his room. He stepped forward and offered me his arm in a crook, it reminded me of doing the same with my Granny, it was the fourth time in as many months that I'd seen him. I sat down, then he sat down, and that's when he said to me in a gentle, patient tone: *Take your time.* My fingers held a biro and hovered over a question on a sheet of paper that he'd handed me – a mental health questionnaire – I had to circle a number between one and ten to rate myself about things like my lack of energy and feelings of hopelessness and thoughts about suicide and it was at that point that I said to the Doctor I know I don't have the bottle to commit suicide, but that doesn't mean that I'm not done with life; I ask the Good Lord to take me quietly in my sleep. I laughed at the sound of my own voice and the sentences I'd pathetically strung together. Doctor

Morgan nodded seriously, next thing I remember my head is on the desk, and I didn't know when my bawling would stop, I remember my stomach muscles still painful a few days later because of the ferocity of my sobbing.

Show me these pills, then? Tall Paul asks, so I toss him the box over the pub table. I take my orange Clipper and light up again, watching him study the writing on the small cardboard packet. *What happens if I have to wake you up?* I tell him that if it's an emergency, grab me by the lapels and haul me off the coach. *What if it isn't an emergency, just a pit-stop?* I tell him it's probably best to just let me sleep. *What if you're spark out and it's time for a Pot Noodle?* I tell him to buy me one and replace the foil cover back over the top, I'd rather eat a cold Pot Noodle than miss out on my food. Tall Paul laughs, shakes his head again and repeats: *Twelve hours on a coach. Minimum.* I look at the time on my phone and tell Tall Paul I'm going to get some cigarettes to tide me over until the duty free on the ferry, I ask him if he wants anything, he runs his hand over his small rucksack that rests by his near empty pint glass and says he's got all he needs. I cross Lillie Road and turn to take a photo with my phone of the scene outside the Prince of Wales – flags with emblems, fans in colours drinking pints, fans not in colours doing the same, laughter on the breeze. I cross back over the road and pop into the newsagent for a pack of menthol cigs, telling myself again that I'll stop smoking after the summer, small steps and all that, life is a marathon not a sprint. Stepping out of the shop, I spontaneously turn left instead of right, which would take me back to the pub. I nod at a couple of familiar faces drinking outside the Wee Imp and walk over the bridge, stopping opposite West Brompton station. I lean back against the wall and light a cigarette; the traffic slows before me because of roadworks slightly up ahead past the cemetery by Finborough Road. Between the noise of engines and the splutters of exhausts and the rat-a-tat-tat of a pneumatic drill, the sound of singing reaches my ears, it tugs at something inside, something in my spirit, I can't identify what, now tears spring from my eyes without warning, I don't really give a fuck because I'm used to it now, I wipe my eyes with my sleeve, pull my menthols out of my breast pocket and light a fresh one from the glowing cherry of my current cigarette, chain-smoking now.

The busker's dark skin almost shines. It's magnified by the stark contrast to his patterned shirt, splodges of white mix with egg yolk yellow and egg yolk orange – I picture my daughter kneeling on a chair next to me in the kitchen, I pass her an egg and she breaks it in the bowl with a squeal, passes the empty shell back to me which I toss in the large, empty ice-cream container we use for the compost. I pass her a second egg, she breaks this in the bowl and says: *This one is more orangier, Daddy!* And I reply: *Orange. This yolk is more orange*, and she laughs, repeating: *Orangier, Dad!* I see her with a fork whisking the eggs in the bowl, yellow yolk and orange yolk mixing into one puddle of gloop. I pour a little milk in, she drops the fork and clutches the base of the milk carton to help me, then she goes back to whisking her scrambled eggs; now through the water in my eyes the blur of the busker's shirt starts to lessen, a backdrop of the white and the yellow and the orange stand out in contrast to the grime of the outdated station wall. Impatient drivers with their right elbows resting by their car window glance at him as he sings, dreadlocks sway as he tilts his head back, his whole body leaning back – *LEAN BACK* – yes, his whole body leans as he sings, he has a red bandana fixed neatly over his forehead and tied in a smart knot behind his ears, his eyes are closed, his hands holding his guitar as he leans – *LEAN BACK* – I notice a silver ring in his nose and a silver stud in his ear; it briefly reflects the sun's rays as he turns, his voice is high, I'm no musician – I'm no vocalist – but if your eyes are closed and you're listening to his voice, you'd think this was a girl singing – makes no difference to me either way, I tilt my head and listen to his words: *You will never leave – your love sustaining me, before I even knew what love was....* I stand transfixed, the lyrics piercing something deep in my being. A pedestrian hurries briskly past me, shoving an empty sandwich packet in the bin next to me, it makes me think of ditching personal rubbish, but I don't know how *....You've brought me here to rest – and given me space to breathe –* as goose bumps form over my arms, my chest heaves, I see my head on my Doctor's desk and a bowl of scrambled eggs that my daughter is whisking with delight *....So I'll stay still until it sinks in –* and I repeat in my head *stay still until it sinks in stay still until it sinks in stay still until it sinks in –* then in that moment my body shifts, I want to curl up and sleep, the feeling is overwhelming, so I try to crouch down leaning against the wall but my legs give way and I'm on my knees and then I hear the violin accompanying the guitar but I can't see where it's coming from, maybe the violinist has been out of sight to the side of the busker, for all I know they could be playing their violin right next to me: *I will lean back in the loving arms of a beautiful Father....* And I'm holding my daughter. *.... Breathe deep and know that He is good....* I am holding my son *.... He's a love like no other....* Josie is cradling me *.... And you will never leave, your love sustaining me....* I manage to shift position again to sit down on the pavement against the wall with the bin to my right .... *Before I even knew what love was, you've brought me here to rest....* the lit cigarette rolls redundantly out from between my fingers, I put my arms across my knees .... *and given me space to breathe....* I bury my forehead into the crook of my elbow .... *so I'll stay still until it sinks in....* A peace floods me, I put my palms face up, my arms still crossed over each other .... *now I can see your love is better than all the others that I've seen....* I feel two hands placed in mine; I close my palms over them wondering who it is holding me .... *I am breathing deep all of your goodness, your loving kindness to me....* I open my eyes and see my tears on the pavement .... *I will lean back in the loving arms of a beautiful Father....* I sniff the gathered mucus up my nose and back down my throat, I look up to see who is holding my hands; there is no-one there, and then I hear my phone ringing.

Tall Paul is asking where I am. I tell him I went for a walk, he said he's tried me three times, I said I was sorry, I'd zoned out, not heard the calls, I tell him I'll be two minutes, I'm just by the Wee Imp and he says he'll wait outside The Prince. I cut the call and go to cross the road to give the busker some money, maybe tell him that I like his egg yolk shirt, see what the violinist looks like, but as I wait for a gap in the traffic to cross, I can't see anyone outside the station, and I can't hear any singing or playing, either. I walk on. Paul is waiting on the pavement outside the pub, he looks all concerned. I wonder what's bothering him, and then I realise it's me. I tell him I'm tired, I need to sleep. Making our way down Seagrave Road I keep my eyes steady studying the rich, glorious colours of the flowers in their hanging baskets outside the Atlas pub. As the carpark comes into view, countless coaches are lined up, I try to count them but I feel a bit giddy, I reach out to Paul who steadies me, I'm almost walking in pigeon steps. He asks me if I want to sit down; I whisper: *Let's get on the coach, bruv* and luckily this doesn't take long, he hands our documents to a lady with a fluorescent yellow bib on grasping an important looking clipboard. I don't remember getting on the coach, but I do remember murmuring to Paul to text George when we leave to let him know we're on the way to Maidstone. I mumble something about Friday afternoon traffic being a fucking pain, Paul tells me to take it easy, he'll wake me when we need to get on the ferry, not sure what's gonna happen with passport control, then I hear him calling his wife in hushed tones, his wife also my big sister.

I slept without dreaming.

An announcement on the ferry instructs all passengers to return to the vehicles. I follow George back towards the coach, Tall Paul behind me so I'm sandwiched in the middle, I've got no idea what level or what area of that level the coach is parked in, but George knows, it's stored upstairs in his brain in vast memory banks, he taps the side of his head with his forefinger to illustrate the point. I'd sat outside at the rear of the ferry, George and Paul sunk a few quick pints before coming to sit with me. George had impressively chatted away with a cluster of French students in their native tongue, a few of the girls giggling at his poor, yet earnest, pronunciation of occasional words. I'd not noticed them; I'd been watching the sea and the sky and the birds. I'd slept all the way to the ferry until Paul had rocked me on the shoulder until I stirred, telling me everyone had to vacate their vehicles so I'd have to wake up and get moving. He led me along corridors to the back of the ferry, he pushed through a stiff door and I found a faded bucket seat to plant myself in; I sat in the fresh air with cigarettes and bottled water watching the ocean churn and turn in the wake of the Brittany ferry as it made its familiar bee-line for Calais.

George stops at the front of our coach. I notice the driver for the first time, he's speaking in Welsh to his two colleagues, the three of them running this coach, two of them taking the driving in stints. The younger lad with them, the Cymru Kid, will be fulfilling the drinks orders and pouring boiling water into Pot Noodles, wedging white disposable plastic cutlery into the snack containers, charging over-the-odds for this instant meal. I tell them I'll be demolishing a couple of Chicken and Mushroom's along the way, the Cymru Kid gives me a thumbs up while the driver laughs and tells us that some of the other coaches are held up at Dover, some haven't even left SW6 yet, we're the lucky ones, first out of the block, George says: *Thank God for that* and the co-driver nods towards George and says: *Imagine if y'still stuck at Maidstone services, like* and we all nod in agreement and, noticing a swan air freshener dangling on the dashboard, I say: *You all Swansea, then?* And they reply in unison: *Aye, Jacks, man* followed by: *Fifty quid to sit in your end, eh? Fuck that!* and we all laugh because we hear it all the time, daylight robbery, but that's modern football for you; Chelsea's prices amongst the highest.

I tell Paul I'll take the window seat, because he'll be needing a piss, no doubt. George sits in front of him, all bouncy and fidgety, three pints in with a thirst, looks up and points to a lad with a Mohican, all shaved bald a grade zero at the back and sides except for a messy brown mop on the top, George stands straight back up and jests: *He cuts his own hair! He cuts his own hair! Raul Meireles, he cuts his own hair!* The lad blushes a bit, he's wearing that white away kit I love – like a packet of Embassy mild – Veron burying a beauty at Anfield on the first day of the 2003/04 season – George goes over to him and shakes his hand, they get chatting, George offers him a sly can from his bag, asking: *Travel candy, mate?* The lad accepts – he's has got a new coach buddy now – George says to him: *Don't tell me your name, I'm calling you Raul.* I settle into my seat, (platinum), and fiddle with my headphones, untangling white wires before slotting the jack into the socket. Placing a sleeping pill on my tongue, I unscrew the plastic blue top off my bottle and sip it down, it will take about an hour for the sedative to kick in. Before I select 'airplane mode' on my phone, I open a text that's dropped in from my Southampton-loving mate, Blanco: *Pulled a right sort from Madrid! Tanned figure and voluptuous chest (.) (.) But she's got a nose like Matt Le Tissier! After drinking a couple of bottles of Freixenet Prosecco and a pack of Estrella Galicia's, it soon straightened itself up* ☺

Laughter is the best medicine. I hand Paul my phone to show him and he duly cracks up. Something occurs to me, so I stand and kneel on my seat and say hello to the bloke sat behind me. I ask him if he's okay if I recline my seat, please. I explain to him my body-clock is all over the place and I'll probably drop off in the next hour and sleep until Germany. He says: *No worries, mate. No problem at all.* I sit back and pull the black lever, platinum seat in full recline mode, move my blue pillow onto my right shoulder and look out the window. I study the movements out of the glass as the coach drives into Calais, I hear George and Raul chatting, the familiar sound of another can opening follows, Paul's back on the phone to my big sister, someone at the front sings: *We're All Going on a European Tour,* seagulls flap, dive and swirl under ominous grey clouds, I press play to start listening to my thirty-eight minute meditation, I'm not sure if I even last ten minutes, Paul tells me the next morning that I was spark straight out.

Then the visions began.

Chapter Eight

COACH DREAMS

Friday night / Saturday morning

My blue and white coloured dingy is a perfect fit, it's got a plush Chelsea-Pensioner-red trim around the edge. The lion holding a staff (the Earl of Cadogan's coat of arms) is emblazoned on the base of the boat – my legs are stretched out over the Chelsea badge, staff and tongue coloured in a rich red to match the trim around the dinghy. Two blue stars sit either side of the badge – it's a precise replica of the 1984 – 1986 Le Coq Sportif kit, and I'll be sailing down the river in it. I think of the Latin motto on the 1903 coat of arms, two years before Chelsea Football Club was formed: *NISI DOMINUS FRUSTRA* – WITHOUT GOD ALL IS IN VAIN. I rest an arm over each side, I'm leant back on an inflatable patch of shiny silver, (the only part of my dinghy that isn't blue, white or red), my reclined spine cushioned comfortably against it. I seem to be amongst a multitude of inflatable dinghies, we are all softly bobbing down the river at the mercy of its (now gentle) current, smiles and laughter fill the air. I hear my name being called, I swivel my head sharply to the left, Ed Sokolowski is grinning from ear to ear, he's raising an open carton of Sangria in the air to toast the occasion. His boat is the same as mine! However, along the side of his dinghy, written in Chelsea-Pensioner-red is the title: *FINNISH BEER FLOATING CHAMPION!* I shout at him: *You're the Champion mate!* And he says: *Told you you'd love the beer floating!* I call out to Ed: *Has my dinghy got a name?* And he looks down, scanning along the side of my boat. He smiles and yells: *ATOMIC 78!* I reply with a shrug: *What does that mean?* And he explains: *ATOMIC 78? It's the chemical number for platinum!* I salute Ed as he slowly overtakes me; he turns with a grin to expertly lob an unopened, chilled carton of Sangria into my dinghy, it lands right between my knees, destined to be opened forthwith. As the current takes Ed ahead of me, I notice that he's got a bag clipped to the rear of his dinghy, it's full of cartons of the drink, the cold, rushing water keeping the drink cooler than if he had them resting by his feet in the boat. I recline back into the shiny, silver platinum seat of *ATOMIC 78*.

The sides of the river are a mixture of slated rock accompanying sandy soil, topped off with long, rich, green grass – the bank rises and dips like a roller coaster. Where the rock subsides to ground level, there's intermittent spaces, (small bays), for people to access the water's edge. Bunches of folk are funneling down from the fields they've crossed, eager to get to the bays to cluster and push off. It's the perfect spot to launch. Lads are carrying dinghies with their pals in a chain, the front of one boat in one hand, the other hand holding the end of another boat, each boat a different colour – they are following the person in front who is following the person in front – a rainbow troop snaking down to their destination. It's quite a spectacle, I wish I had a camera. A girl is carrying four oars, two under each arm, they stick out at varying angles making it awkward for her to balance, the rucksack she has over both shoulders full of food and drink, no doubt. As I float past their location from where they'll soon launch, the mid-morning sun peeks out from behind cotton wool clouds, it's going to be a magnificent day once the clouds have fully cleared, which they hopefully will. The riverbank rocks rise again. A stag raises its head from the grass and looks at me, chewing absentmindedly, its antlers reminding me of the girl with oars under her arms, the huge sturdy extension of the stag's skull oozes a tangible presence of authority. A small herd of deer appear either side of him with twitching noses and inquisitive eyes, their white tails momentarily bobbing in rhythm with my inflatable dinghy. When they finish their brief study of me, they move their heads back down to continue munching on the grass. I think of the change in seasons when the snow will come – blizzards blowing across Scandinavia; the stags and deer slowly crunching through snow, heads down, cold noses shifting flakes to reveal the green they need. I hear a *whump-thump-whump*; it gets louder as it gets closer – *WHUMP-THUMP-WHUMP* – I look up. Incredibly, a blanket of white soars across my line of vision. Two whooper swans cruise only a few feet above me! Their routine has been disrupted by the beer-floating festival – their wingspan can reach up to 2.8 metres – they won't be diving for any aquatic plants or roots until the morning when the mass of boats, beer and human beings have gone. The sound of their beating wings becomes softer as they fly further downstream. I keep my eyes on them until they bank right and disappear into trees, far into the distance; I zone out for a bit now, stunned by the closeness of their bodies flying above me in my boat. Time passes; my solace is broken when the familiar cry of a young Welsh voice behind me shouts: *Fancy a Pot Noodle, mate?*

Craning to my left, I see a black and white dinghy approaching quickly behind me, I laugh a *hello* at the two coach drivers who crouch on either side of their boat, they each hold an oar, it occurs to me that I'm simply floating, I don't have oars like they do. In the centre of their dinghy, the Cymru Kid raises a Chicken and Chow Mein in my direction, noodles spilling out between his lips, he waves at me as he sucks them up into his mouth and chews with a smile. They're all wearing red life-jackets. Our boats bump together, their white inflatable divided by a ring of black all around it – it's the colours of their football team – Swansea City. One of the drivers points his oar to the horizon and says: *See the swans flying, did you?* I nod and he produces a coin. Placing it between his thumb and forefinger, he flicks it expertly into the air. I watch it rise, gold glistening in the sun as it spins higher. When it drops, I reach out my hand and catch the coin. Beautifully engraved on one side are two whooper swans, elegant necks stretched forward; one's wings are up above its body, the others swan's wings low down – they are moving above land and water – I turn the coin over – it's a Finnish one Euro – the whooper swans are their emblem. Thrusting his oar towards the horizon, the second driver instructs me: *When the River splits, go right. Don't miss it. Trust me – take the narrow way.* I nod my reply as they continue to bump-float past me, the sides of our boats still touching, almost locked together. I'm about to flick the coin back to the first driver, but he shakes his head, ordering: *Keep it, ATOMIC 78, you'll need it.* He takes his oar, places it on the side of my dinghy and pushes away, the maneuver thrusts me back sending ripples skipping up over the side whilst simultaneously propelling them downstream. With their backs to me now, the coach drivers dip their oars into the water and drive them determinedly down in unison, their symmetrical power thrusting them forward. The Cymru Kid turns and raises his hand to give me a thumbs up. The name of their vessel jumps out at me – *LIBERTY* – of course! Swansea City play their home games in the Liberty Stadium. I drop the Finnish Euro in my breast pocket and button it up to keep it safe, I pat the whooper swans frozen in metal, feeling the cold coin pressing against my chest through the material of my shirt. Once more, I recline back in my platinum seat. As I look at the water and sky, I make a mental list of the definitions of

LIBERTY; I run through as many meanings as I can: *independence; freedom; autonomy; sovereignty; free reign; license; non-coercion; birthright; dispensation; carte blanche* – ha, I like *carte blanche* – it means *complete freedom.* Floating gently downstream, the riverbank dominates my eye-line; I smile at the smooth slates of rock – they've had the flow of water lapping over them for centuries; gently massaging the stone for millennia, slowly making them smoother than silk, I'm reminded of the wave-cut-platform at Dancing Ledge and George's speech explaining the history of the area – I have absolutely no idea of time, I'm in the shallows caught in the wonder of the smooth stones and pebbles – I'm oblivious to dinghys both large and small holding either groups or individuals floating past me, it creates a perfect background noise of joy as all the occupants are in such high-spirited moods.

I have no idea how many minutes or even hours have passed – I'm suddenly aware that the temperature has dropped significantly, my arms are chilled, I try and warm the goosebumps away by rubbing my hands vigorously up and down my arms; I'm unsuccessful. I'm cold. Very cold. I lean over the side and put my arms in the water, feel for a large stone to firmly push off to get my dinghy moving from the shallows. I launch into the centre of the river now, it's eerily quiet, there are no other vessels, no people, no laughter, no human noise at all, just the panicked cry of birds as they head for the hills.

In the distance to my right I can make out the silhouette of a figure on the riverbank next to the edge of a pine forest. He is waving, both arms held high in the air, crossing them back and forth, I'm intrigued, there's no need to urge *ATOMIC 78* forward to see who this is, because the current increases rapidly, I'm suddenly travelling far too fast for my own comfort, to be honest. I shift forward to kneel. Pushing my back straight, I raise my arms to mimic the wave – it's then that my heart jumps! It's a familiar stance, a familiar wave! Is it Moon? Ha! Is it? It must be – it's the same crisscross wave we exchanged as we said *goodbye* in Valencia. My joy is short-lived, however – my elation robbed from me – a biting cold wind rushes in against my body as a thud of water slaps against the side of my dinghy rocking me to the side. Still kneeling, I regain my balance by grabbing the sides of the dinghy, the wind picks up, even stronger now, it swirls around me, I'm reminded of flying empty crisp packets in the corner of the playground being whipped in circles by an invisible force as a storm closes in – cold, biting air is gnawing viciously at my skin like an irritated, wailing red-cheeked toddler crunching their sore gums into a teething ring; what's left of the failing sun disappears in seconds. I look up at billowing, ominous, clouds – streaks of black cloud dash the sky like an oil spill of marmite smeared thickly on a canvas – Moon is waving more avidly now, I realise his waving is not a welcome but a warning, his black polo shirt matching the ever-darkening sky. Moon stops crisscrossing his arms – now he holds them outstretched – he is sweeping them both in unison in a motion from the river to the side – more rough water slaps the side of my dinghy, the carton of Sangria is rolling up and down like an empty beer bottle on the floor of a coach on an away trip – I realise I've frozen a little bit, unsure what to do, the weather has changed in an instant like the warnings you get before climbing Welsh mountains like Snowdon or Tryfan or Pen Y Fan – it's inexplicable – I'm not prepared at all. Churning waves slap the boat harder, everything above is now dark grey to black, the wind is gale-force now, the younger forest trees behind Moon are bending like the spine of a hunchback; *oh fuck*…. I realise Moon is using the sweeping motion of his arms to try to tell me to get out of the centre of the river and get to the right side to the safety of the bank, the movement of his arms are screaming *GET OUT OF THE WATER* but I've got no oars, I'm at the mercy of the moody, choppy current. Moon starts to run.

I try and think clearly, I know I need to stay to the right, that's what the coach driver advised, but the reality is that I'm near the middle of the river and the current is thundering down and taking me with it, and now the rain starts falling in lumps, crashing and splashing into the river. I hear Moon screaming before I can see him – *GRAB IT! GRAB IT!* – I hear a *WHUMP* as a cowboy rope slams into my dinghy – still on my knees, I grasp it with both hands, quickly wrapping wrists around it like you would for a tug-of-war contest – with my grip firm, I duck into the loop he's made, lassoing myself like an animal – Moon has slung me a calf-rope – I push the nylon over my shoulders and wriggle it down over my waist – as a result, my weight has shifted and my balance compromised, the wind whips *ATOMIC 78* from under me. Still holding the rope, I'm dumped into freezing water, the dinghy capsizes acrobatically over and rises in the wind like a disfigured hot air balloon – the Earl of Cadogan's coat of arms flips like a spinning top; bouncing on the water and propelled by the storm, it flies downstream, it's out of sight in seconds, blown and flown over an edge in the distance – maybe the edge of a waterfall, maybe the edge of the world, I don't know, but I know I cannot go further towards the sheer drop. Ed's gift to me of a carton of Sangria now at the mercy of the current, swerving rocks and low-hanging branches before being tossed over the brink, following *ATOMIC 78* to oblivion.

Moon has wrapped and fastened the other end of the rope around a huge pine tree on the riverbank. If I let go of my end, I'm done. On cue, Moon screams through the rain: *DON'T LET GO!* He's dug his heels in and started pulling me towards him, the water is up to my waist and churning around me, always picking up pace as it races towards the edge of the waterfall, (or is it the edge of the world), it occurs to me that it's a fight for my life, I feel like a fool, my teeth chattering hard, I picture a plastic mouth with painted red lips mounted on oversized plastic feet with a key on the side – you wind the key up and the feet start walking, and the teeth start chattering. If I give in, I'll start sinking – *DON'T STAND STILL!* I shrug my shoulders, my hair stuck to my face – *COME ON – COOOOME ON!* Obediently, I put one foot forward, push my body against the current, I lurch backwards again, though – it feels like one step forward and two steps back – *GET A GRIP, YOU MUG* – I don't know if it's Moon howling at me, or me screaming at myself – he's pulling me forward, and I'm pushing myself on. I remind myself that one end of the rope is tied on to a thick trunk of pine, no way that tree is going anywhere. If I slip, though, I'll hang myself – my arms would slip through the lasso causing the noose to would shift up from my waist and tighten around my neck – is it better to go that way, (body floating in the water, current churning around me, one end of the rope on my neck, the other around an ancient pine), or is it better to fall over the edge of the waterfall, (or is it the edge of the world), *God knows* – there's no mistaking Moon's piercing cry, now though: *FIGHT – FIIIIGHT!* So, I start to fucking fight. I roar into the rain, urging myself forward, Moon pulling me in, it takes everything within me and more, fighting against the current, one end of the rope lassoed to a tree, if I flop or fall back, that's probably it, Moon wouldn't be able to take the strain of my body against the storm in the air combined with the thrashing current – *COME ON – COOOOME ON!* Maybe my head or my limbs will swing round in the body of water and bash against an unmerciful boulder – brains smashed against rock – I won't feel a thing – like when you take a chickens head off there's an instant death for the chicken, a finality, it's just the body aggressively twitching for a minute or two that brings a bigger drama than it actually is – I wonder how much my body will twist in the water when my brain is mushed with finality on rock. I won't feel a thing, it'll be like a finger pressing a light switch, and the bulb goes out.... *FIGHT – FIIIIGHT!*

I see Josie with her back to me hanging up the wet laundry on the line, it will be sea-breeze-dried; I see my daughter running towards me across the garden calling DADDY *with her arms open wide; I see my son following her shouting* DAD-DAD-DAD *with a toy car in his hand; I hear the voice of the Lady Who Looks Like My Aunty telling me* ON YOU GO, DEAR, YOU'RE NEARLY ON LAND; *I see the Doctor with a concerned look on his brow; I feel the voice of Jah whispering:* it's not your time to go yet, not now....

NISI DOMINUS FRUSTRA.

I feel two, giant invisible hands shove me to safety as if they're thrusting me off a train track and up on to a platform to save me from a hurtling, oncoming locomotive. I flop on the shore where Moon puts his hands under my armpits and hauls me forward that last little bit before collapsing next to me, blood on his palms from rope burns. The nylon has taken his skin off where he's been desperately hauling me in; blood is smeared over his exhausted face where he's run his bloodied hands over his wet cheeks; it's also covering my torso in patches where he's hauled me up, deposits of his blood splotched over me like port stains on a white table cloth.

The curdling shriek of a wild animal accompanies ear-splitting hungry howls of the wolves – their ravenous cries pierce the air through the sound of the storm: *STEP OUT OF THE CALF ROPE!* Moon screams as he springs up with fright – he's rising from the river bank like a bruised matador. It's a call to action. He runs to the ancient pine and starts furiously untying a double airbed he's got secured there. I step out of the rope and pick it up, as I move towards Moon, he yells above the rain: *TAKE THIS END AND RUN WITH ME!* We have one end of the airbed each, we're running away from the river, it's the right-hand turn that I should have looked out for, the fork in the river, the narrow way that I should have taken, we have to get to the forked section, we have to make it. I look behind me as a pack of wolves sprint out of the pine forest into the clearing arching in a tight corner like speedway motorbikes skidding around a bend of their final lap, one wolf loses his footing on the apex of land and bank and tumbles into the crashing river; as we run I start to laugh at the ridiculousness of it all and Moon starts to laugh, too, adrenaline coursing through our systems once more. Still running, Moon shouts – *I don't have a dinghy, CARTE BLANCHE will do* – and I reply: *Carte Blanche? Eh?* And Moon chuckles – *well, I had to name my airbed, right?* – and then he yells: *JUMP! JUUUUMP!* And we jump off the riverbank holding the top of the bed as if it's a magic carpet. A wolf snaps at our heels and falls to be swept away, with the air bed under us we briefly soar like the wings of a whooper swan before landing on water, me on the right of the bed and Moon on the left – the narrow river we are on is our sanctuary – Moon is gasping, while he catches his breath he pats the bed as if it were a pet and says: *Carte Blanche – complete freedom to act as one wishes* – he adjusts his position and starts kicking with his legs, so I do the same – and Moon says to me that the two of us kicking like this mirrors the final scene in the film *Jaws* when Chief Brody and Hooper are holding on to a plank of wood with two yellow barrels either side of them, they're kicking towards the shore, the dead shark has sunk to the bottom of the Atlantic Ocean, Hooper has got his flippers on, together they propel towards home.

The storm has gone. The rain has stopped. The sky is clear. Stars begin to appear. The pine forest to our left looms high, the clearing to our right is dotted with people around warm camp fires, it's the end of the beer-floating route – I hear Ed calling my name, he's waving at me from the riverbank, he says: *You finally made it, then! Now the Kaljakellunta route is complete, the festival will finish with a short concert!* I give Ed a thumbs up, Moon and I stop kicking as we reach the bank where Larry is waiting with two deckchairs, one for me and one for Moon, each of them striped blue and white with a Chelsea-Pensioner-red trimming. Larry points towards George who is fully reclined, lent back, in his matching deckchair snoring softly in his familiar sleeping posture: Arms crossed, hands tucked under his arm pits, eyes closed, mouth open. Larry has got a strong camp-fire on the go – Tall Paul is in his matching deckchair staring contentedly into the flames. Larry motions to the dry logs piled between our deckchairs to add when needed, while handing us towels to dry ourselves. Moon takes the rope and secures *Carte Blanche* to the trunk of a nearby lone pine tree so it won't blow away. Two whooper swans fly overhead and land on the opposite bank. They flap their wings and settle, nuzzling their beaks into their sides. The humming noise of the multitudes chatting quickly hushes as the sound of a guitar tuning fills the air. I look up to the stage, along the side is a string of lanterns. Each one is lit, the case covering each lantern is a different colour. On the stage is no other than the busker from outside West Brompton train station! He's wearing a blue shirt, unbuttoned, that covers a white t-shirt. He has a Chelsea-Pensioner-red bandana fastened around his forehead; the curls of his afro fringe slightly hang over the bandana. A silver cross on a silver chain hangs delicately around his neck. It complements the silver ring in his nostrils and the silver stud in his ear. Larry leans into me and says all proudly: *My Liz is singing with that fella today* and I smile knowing it's going to be beautiful. I know their voices will deeply move all who listen; each and every soul will connect with Jah; Mother Nature surrounding all like a secure blanket. Liz appears next to the busker on the stage – she wears a blue sleeveless pinafore dress that hugs her petite figure, a white t-shirt underneath. She has Chelsea-Pensioner-red lipstick on that perfectly matches her heels. A silver cross on a silver chain hangs delicately around her neck. It complements the silver hoops in her ears. Liz and the busker meekly accept the applause from the audience, there's a child-like innocence about them as they smile at each other – a shyness, almost, that they're on a stage – you can feel the air of humility radiating from them. Larry points at each of our Chelsea deckchairs and says: *You can lean back well comfortably in these, lads* before doing exactly that. I lean back in mine. Moon arranges three fresh logs on the fire, I notice his hands are bandaged up, then he sits down to lean back in his deckchair, too. *LEAN BACK.* The busker begins to play his guitar and then he and Liz sing. *Lean Back:*

You will never leave / Your love's sustaining me / Before I even knew what love was / You've brought me here to rest / And given me space to breathe / So, I'll stay still until it sinks in / I will lean back in the loving arms / Of a beautiful Father / Breathe deep and know that He is good / He's a love like no other / And You will never leave / Your love's sustaining me / Before I even knew what love was / You've brought me here to rest / And given me space to breathe / So, I'll stay still until it sinks in / I will lean back in the loving arms / Of a beautiful Father / Breathe deep and know that He is good / He's a love like no other / Now I can see / Your love is better / Than all the others / That I've seen / I'm breathing deep / All of your goodness / And your loving kindness to me / Now I can see / Your love is better / Than all of the others / That

LET THE CELERY DECIDE

I've seen / I'm breathing deep / All of your goodness / Your loving kindness to me / I will lean back in the loving arms of a beautiful Father / Breathe deep and know that He is good / He's a love like no other / You will never leave / Your love's sustaining me / Before I even knew what love was....

Through the applause of the crowd, I hear the unmistakable Welsh tones of the Cymru Kid – I look up and see he's pointing at me telling Tall Paul that I have to pay for my food. I open the button of my breast pocket and fish out the Finnish Euro – the Cymru Kid laughs at me and nods – I lean forward in my deckchair and flick the coin up in the air over to him, he watches it spinning towards him, he catches it with precision and pockets his payment before giving me a thumbs up. He hands Tall Paul a Chicken and Mushroom Pot Noodle for me. As the crowd's applause lessens for Liz and the busker, shouts of *ENCORE!* fill the atmosphere. Everyone in the audience is hungry for another song. I'm hungry for food. Famished. Tall Paul brings my instant snack over, the white plastic cutlery sticking out over the pot, this will fill a gap in my rumbling tummy, keep me going until the coach arrives in Munich, no doubt.

Chapter Nine

MUNICH

Saturday 19th May 2012

I open my eyes, stretch out the stiffness in my neck, reach down to my right and fiddle for the black handle. I give it a yank and my reclining seat, (platinum), jumps back into its original position. In front of me, on my small, white, plastic tray, sits a glorious Chicken and Mushroom Pot Noodle. The foil lid has been thoughtfully placed back over the top to keep the warmth in, the handle of a piece of white, plastic cutlery is sticking out of a gap in the foil. Hot steam rises and Tall Paul says to me: *Morning, there's your breakfast. You were spark out.* I rub my eyes and look around, the Cymru Kid is about to step back to the stairs to the lower deck when he looks up and grins: *Wakey-wakey, Chelsea.* As he descends, I reply: *Morning, Swansea* and he gives me a thumbs up. Two whooper swans soar in my mind's eye causing my tongue to stick in my mouth, a lump forms in my throat; I turn to Paul and I'm about to tell him about this fragment of my vivid dream but I can't get my words out, besides, Paul leans forward and slaps George on the shoulder. He turns to tell us that he reckons he smells like the changing room after Rugby in the sixth form and then he adds: *Half-hour until Munich.* I realise there's an air of anticipation that's built up here on the coach, and right on cue one of the drivers comes over the tannoy system to announce our impending arrival – everyone cheers – he gives us the details we've heard before, and he signs off by shouting: *Up the Jacks!* (slight boos resound) followed by: *Good luck, Chelsea – you better fuckin' win or our journey home will be a fuckin' nightmare, eh?* Everyone laughs and then someone at the back yells: *We are the famous, the famous Chelsea!* (four claps). The whole coach sings: *We are the famous, the famous Chelsea!* Then a deep voice from the front growls a phrase we'll hear intermittently for the next sixteen hours as the day and then the match-drama unfolds: *Come on, Chelsea!*

Each with a fresh shirt on, we pile off the coach into the morning Munich sunshine. We've parked up near the Allianz Arena, George cocks his head in the direction of the ground, we dutifully walk through the big, open white gates of the car park and towards the ground. The morning heat is welcome, Paul says it's twenty degrees already, and George smiles and remarks that it's perfect drinking weather. On the way to the stadium, plenty are mingling about already. A middle-aged balding man in a Bayern shirt is holding a large cardboard sign asking for a spare ticket. He could be a chauffeur in an airport foyer, nonchalantly leaning against a rail holding the name of the passenger on the card between his fingers; eyes darting around looking for a response as travellers file though the exits with their baggage. George asks him how much he'd be willing to pay and he smiles and says: *Maybe up to one thousand Euros!* The enthusiasm in his accent reminds me of a German teacher we had at school, her name was Mrs. Fama, I think she was brought up in Italy, but I can't be sure. She taught Spanish and French as well as her native tongue, (no doubt spoke Italian too), and she was one of the good guys. I was absolutely terrible at languages, that part of my brain so obviously redundant, but her classroom was a sanctuary. I must have been one of her worst students when it came to learning an additional language, but she clearly separated this when it came to our physical and mental health. We could hang out in there at lunchtime when we were in the lower school, away from the kickings and the slaps from the older lads. She would munch on her sandwiches, too. Years later I reflected on why she wouldn't be in the staff room, it must've been because she didn't get on with everyone, maybe she was teased – or bullied, even, for her nationality.

I study the Allianz Arena, about seven years old now, and I remark that the white ring encompassing the stands and pitch reminds me of the Michelin Man from the tyre adverts. Nodding in agreement, George points at it and says: *Schlauchboot!* Tall Paul looks at me and says: *He's speaking in tongues again.* George smiles and repeats: *Schlauchboot!* I roll my eyes in jest as brain-box of the decade explains that the Arena is famously known for its unique exterior made up of inflated panels. I tell him he must be joking, and he says: *Nah – 'schlauchboot' is the stadium's nickname – it means 'dinghy'.* As he says the word *dinghy,* I see *ATOMIC 78* in my dream flipping furiously, the angry wind has whipped it from under me and sent it spinning downstream. As we make our way around the metal security barriers, circling around back to where we came from, I explain to the lads about Ed telling me about the Finnish beer-floating festival, all the participants in inflatable dinghies. (I keep my thoughts to myself about my dreams in the night.) George's eyes widened: *A beer-floating festival? In Finland?* He is absolutely buzzing, he keeps peppering me with questions, demanding I tell him more, I just tell him what Ed told me, and that the name *Kalijakellunta* essentially translates 'Kalja' is beer, and 'Kellunta' is floating. He scratches the beard on his chin, and then flicks his finger over his nose before he exclaims: *Let's do it for your fortieth birthday!* Tall Paul changes the subject saying he needs breakfast, he's well hungry, and we all agree. My currywurst with a side of French fries last about three minutes, so I order another one, washing it all down with a large cardboard cup of Coke, a white, paper straw sticking through the gap in the plastic lid. George pulls some toothpaste, travel deodorant and a pack of baby-wipes out of his small, black sports bag. I pull my toothbrush out of the front pocket of my jeans and pick out the fluff from the bristles. We all have a trucker's wash at the sinks in the bogs using the wipes; once clean, our armpits all have a blast from George's spray. *Don't use the wipes on your arse,* George warns; *You'll get a proper rash on your crevice.* Sound advice. *Was camping once, no bog roll in the Gents, used a wipe or three and then spent two days in discomfort with a rash. Worse than piles.* Paul says we'd better get a move on; we have to return to the coach-park – this time to meet Taxi Alan, Vastly Intelligent Keef, Champagne Les and Mascot Tommy who are on the official club trip. After landing at Munich Airport, coaches are ferrying them to the same car park. Mascot Tom has sent a text to Paul to say they've landed and are on the transfer coach, it's a twenty-minute journey. It's perfect timing. As we cross the street towards the big, open white gates, they're all disembarking and, it goes without saying, they've got a raging thirst on. Tom says two fellas on their flight went to get a beer after landing, the bus had to leave, so it went without them. Problem is, you didn't get your match ticket until you were checked in on the bus. The mention of beer gets everyone licking their lips. It's just about finding the right boozer, hoping luck and spontaneity collide, we all march south to the nearest station – Fröttmaning on the U6 line – Champagne Les says that on the map, the U6 lines is coloured Chelsea blue – it will take us into Munich for booze and food, and then back to the ground for kick-off. I look at the map – Les is right, it is the colour of Chelsea blue.

We travel ten stops south to Odeonsplatz and walk through and around the huge square. It occurred to me that I could group all the types of people into five sets. Firstly, German citizens. Secondly, standard tourists. Thirdly, locals working in their day jobs. Fourthly, Bayern fans and finally; thirsty Chelsea supporters. Intermittent cries of *Baaayern! Baaayern!* could be heard as we moved around the square – a cry that would ultimately get more and more under my skin as the day unravelled. The Manchester United of Germany. Arrogant and self-entitled. Proper Munich football lovers follow the blue of Munich 1860. A rampant lion on their badge; formed in a pub in 1848 (sound familiar?), they won the league for the only time in 1965/66 – this season they've finished in a respectable sixth place. They're all Chelsea tonight. We left the Odeonsplatz to walk a few blocks south to Marienplatz where we settle in the beer garden of a gaff called Augustiner am Dom. We had to walk across its long bar and restaurant, wooden floor under my trainers, the huge patio doors were pulled open and locked in position, although a long section of glass separated the bar and restaurant from the garden. I realise Champagne Les isn't with us anymore – Keef says he's met some other pals; we'll hook back up with him later. Soon, our table is full of plates of Wiener Schnitzel with sides of potato salad and French fries, baskets of fresh bread and steins of Augustiner – two glorious pints in one unique glass. I stick to Coke, it's getting boring now, but I'm at peace with it, the alternative is not currently an option. I sit in the sun smoking, I'll need another pack soon, turning my trusty orange Clipper in my hand, I marvel that I haven't mislaid it over all these weeks. The beer garden has filled up nicely, mostly Chelsea with a few clusters of red Bayern shirts in a group or two tucking into their lunch, we agree to stick here for the day, no point in moving to try and find another gaff, thousands of Chelsea have, and are, descending on the City. I need a piss, Mascot Tom directs me to where it is; past the bar, go straight on, turn right – so through the patio door I go. A cheer greets me – *Oi Oi, Walts!* Sitting around a table engulfed by steins of Augustiner are a few of the boys: The Sherman Chef, Lorch, Shane, Bourne, Percy, Joe the Fiddler, Ross, Papa G and Fingers. Lorch says: *Of all the boozers in Munich, and you walk into this one.* Covering a painting, their huge Union Jack flag is fixed to the wall behind them, CHELSEA written in white across the middle – there's a space at the head of the table next to Lorch, I tell them I'll be two minutes. They offer me a drink, but I decline, I tell them I'm on antibiotics of sorts and Fingers shouts to me: *Caught a dose in Barca, did ya?* And everyone has a laugh. I spread my hands out wide, palms up, point at my wedding ring and say with a smile: *There's only one for me, boys* and I know that they don't know if I'm serious or not, but Lorch knows that I am. I first met Fingers Tom at Goodison Park. I'd been in the upper tier and was making my way down the stairs for a half-time pint or two. I can see Lorch leaning against the wall with a couple of pals, all of them with a pint in their hand, no doubt been on it all day, shots and all. I call down to him and he waves, he introduces me to Tom who has his free hand down the front of his trousers, rearranging his bollocks. I instinctively put my hand out to shake his – he removes his hand from his pants, sniffs his fingers, wiggles them under my nose and then shakes my hand. That's how he got his nickname.

Exiting the toilet, the bar is three deep now, I snake through the thirsty crowd, people shifting their weight from one foot to the other, the bar staff are looking flustered already, the day has hardly begun. The duty manager wipes his brow with the back of his hand, beads of sweat transferred to his white sleeve, he'll be rolling them up in no time as the establishment becomes hotter still. The seat is still available next to Lorch, I sit down and we have a catch-up. I first met him and his Dad years before on a train back from Wigan. I tell him about my journey, that me and George and Paul don't have tickets. We chat about Barcelona. I tell him briefly about my health, ask him to keep it to himself for now, the less people that know, the better, just don't know how long I'll be like this, but right now everything is brilliant – I'm here and I'm happy, and the moment is all I need. Much later giddiness might appear, anxiety may rain down and drowsiness prevail – it does most days, but I've got George and Paul with me just like Larry was with me for the trip to Valencia and Barca. I watched the FA Cup Final in bed – the only time I got up that day was to go to the bogs, but I'm here now, aren't I?

The first *Caaaaaarefreeeeee!* of the day belts out from the beer garden to my left, it carries through the open porch doors and catches on, many in the three-deep queue warm up their vocal cords. The songs continue: *One Team in London! Double Double Double!* And *Oh West London is Wonderful!* A Bayern fan has politely pushed his way through the queueing mass, his friends obviously residing in the beer garden. The bloke, in his fifties, is a giant – got to be six foot six at least. He has a black leather bikers' waistcoat over an old, faded denim shirt. His long grey hair is kind of plaited in parts, some braided with beads – it's the same with his long beard – it's plaited under his chin, a selection of beads threaded in, too. A red bandana is tied over his head, both ears pierced multiple times displaying silver studs and hoops alike. *Excuse me; please; Danke* he softly repeats as he manoeuvres through the crowd, then someone behind him shouts: *One Jack Sparrow! There's only one Jack Sparrow!* About three hundred people simultaneously burst out laughing (Captain Jack Sparrow is a fictional pirate played in several films by Johnny Depp) and join in singing at him. As he crosses into the beer garden, he turns and waves with a big grin on his face. Everyone cheers. *Sparrow! Give us a song! Sparrow, Sparrow give us a song!* Smiling broadly, he puffs out his chest and yells: *Baaayern! Baaayern!* A beer mat is used as a Frisbee and flicked towards him, he catches it, (a huge cheer follows), and he throws it back, high into the air, laughing still. Anyone with a beer mat to hand lobs it in his general direction until he steps backwards into the garden in surrender, swatting flying beer mats and laughing still. An overly-flustered barmaid has had enough already. Holding a tray with about eight full steins in she yells: *STOP THROW-EEENG ZEE FUCK-EEENG BEER MATZ!* Everyone cheers (again) – in that same *WA-EY* chorus that greets the sound of shattering glass when a bar person drops one on the floor – but the *WA-EY* is amplified about three hundred times; then someone starts singing the Dambusters theme while she angrily tries to find the table that she's delivering the tray full of booze to. In that moment, for some reason a young man with a mop of brown hair and large, full-moon spectacles becomes (slightly) the centre of attention, but I don't know why. A song begins: *One Harry Potter! There's Only One Harry Potter!* He blushes and laughs it off, got no choice really. Whatever way he turns, (looking a little bewildered) people are pointing and serenading him. It goes again: *Potter! Give Us A Spell! Potter, Potter Give Us A Spell!* Followed by fingers on lips: *Shhhhhh... AGGGGGGHHHH!* He looks all right though, taking it in his stride. George appears at our table side, laughing at the ridiculousness of it all. *Shall We Cast A Spell for You! Shall We Cast A Spell for You?* Another song follows: *Expelliarmus! La la la la la la! Expelliarmus! La la la la la la! Expelliarmus! La la la la la laaaaa!* I immediately feel bad as hundreds of lads sing it to him, pointing and raising their steins in his direction. George, perhaps feeling his discomfort (and also being a geeky nerdy Potter fan) starts up: *Oh, Potter We Love You! We Love You Potter, We Do! We Love You Potter, We Do!* The lad is patted on the back and shoulder, we've all a laugh, main thing is he's okay with it, though. A song starts brewing accompanied by steins being banged on the table. It invites more glares from the

Bavarian barmaid. It simply eggs everyone on a little more. From the table that The Sherman Chef oversees, the sound of the base of the glass hitting the wood of the table accompanies a peach of a song, it spreads and catches across the bar and is belted out by the entire boozer for a good ten minutes: *THREE ONE DOWN TO NAPOLI, WHO'D HAVE THOUGHT WE'D BE IN GERMANY? AND NOW WE'RE HERE TO WIN THE CUP, WITHOUT ANELKA TO FUCK IT UP!* (Tune: Tom Hark. Originally an instrumental released in 1958 by Elias & his Zig Zag Jive Flutes, it was covered by The Piranhas in 1980.)

I go back outside for a bit. There are a few older fellas I recognise, those you're on nodding terms with. Vastly Intelligent Keef and Taxi Alan are deep in conversation next to each other, Paul and George sit opposite doing the same. I sit next to Mascot Tommy who is on a picnic table with a few people all kitted out in Bayern red. Tommy introduces me, there's a married couple from Poland and their friend, Frenk. He's an ethnic Albanian from Kosovo, he says his name is the Albanian variation of the good old English name, Frank. We talk for a long time, behind his brown eyes sits the pain of conflict, Tommy welling up and shaking his head as Frenk describes war and atrocities, how his family were ripped apart and how Germany, especially Munich, took him in. He's built a new life, the creases in his brow and the scars on his arms and cheek physical reminders of his old life; the mental scars running deeper still.

Fingers shouts my name from the doorway, he steps forward with Lorch in his wake, they wave me over so I stand up and walk towards them. Fingers takes my elbow and ushers me to the side. *Close your eyes and put your hands out* he says, so I do. He places something light in my hand, like a postcard. *Open your eyes, mush* he says, so I do. I see a barcode, a flash of blue, the European Cup with MUNICH FINAL 2012 written underneath. *It's not a fuckin' photocopy* he grins, as I hold the ticket between my fingers, mouth open. *How much?* I ask. *This is the icing on the cake, bruv – it's free.* I burst out laughing, wondering how the blazes has it come to this, saying *thank you* over and over again. Fingers looks a bit bewildered himself, I ask him if he's okay, ask him why he's giving me a free ticket to the game; ask him to explain what just happened. He exhales and asks me if he smells of puke – I laugh and say he doesn't – I offer him a cigarette, spark up one of my own and give Fingers the time to describe recent events. He puffs his cheeks out and laughs; Lorch tells him to tell me the story, so he does:

It was all pretty rammed downstairs so we went upstairs to get drinks. I was with my pal Andy and his Dad. We got beers and sat down with this random bloke and his son, probably about fifteen or sixteen years old. We were chatting, you know, everyone's having a good time. After a little while, the son came across as being really drunk which was a surprise as he had been fine five minutes before. I got him some water and kept an eye on him but, to my astonishment, he started puking at the table. It was clear he was in a bad way so me, Andy's Dad and this lad's Dad took him outside the bar where there was an alley. We were out there for a while and he was getting worse....

Fingers runs his hand over his head, adjusts his glasses on his nose, and scratches a cheek. I blow smoke out the corner of my mouth, put my right hand under my left armpit and wait for him to continue:

Andy's Dad went back in to sit with Andy, Lorch and the others while I remained outside. Over the next hour or so we made sure he had water and was comfortable but he started puking up black liquid. His Dad told me they had done shots and it's a possibility he'd been spiked. We asked a local to call an ambulance. Which they did. The boy had his head up against the wall and started puking again but then, with his head back, he began choking on the puke and choking on his tongue. I put my hand down his throat and manoeuvred his head down so his tongue would get out the way and he could chunder, which eventually went all over me. As Munich was so busy, it took forever for the ambulance to get there. One Munich fan took a photo of the boy and laughed so I got right up in his face, pushed him and threatened him. He quickly fucked off. His Dad was emotional about it all, as you'd expect, so I comforted him whilst also reassuring the lad as he was understandably feeling pretty bad. All that vomiting seemed to have done the trick as he became a lot more coherent and steadier. Eventually, the ambulance rocked up. They put him on a wheelie bed and I gave the lad a hug and wished him all the best. His Dad gave me a hug and thanked me. He then went into his bag, took out an envelope and handed it to me. I opened it, saw the tickets and asked how much he wanted for them. He said I owed him nothing so I obviously said how grateful I was and that, and I wished him luck. They left and I went back in the boozer and told the boys all about it. I was covered in puke so I asked the bar staff if I could wash up so they led me to a staff area. There was a sink big enough to sit in so I got bollock naked and washed in there! A fit blonde walked in and was pretty shocked seeing an English lad sitting in the sink. I washed my shorts as well as I could, dried up and went back out. That's when I explained everything to the boys at the table just now – then Lorch told me to speak to you, and here we are mate.

There are things I want to ask, but the questions won't formulate. I go to try to remonstrate, but he's having none of it; I mumble something about surely there's another pal he knows who he's been all around the country and Europe with following Chelsea and I think he know what I'm trying to say because he jerks his thumb back towards the table where his pals are still gathered, and says with a finality: *We've all got a ticket, put it in your pocket and be done with it.* And with that he strolls off back into the pub with Lorch behind him. Just like that. I know exactly what I'm doing next. I go over to Tall Paul and George, they're still chatting, oblivious to what has just happened. *Come over here,* I say, and get them into the corner where it's quieter next to a picnic table full of empty steins, lines of froth hardening in the sun around and down the inside of the glass. *Before I start, you both have to agree not to interrupt me, I need to say my piece.* They nod in agreement and Paul says: *Sounds serious.* I point at Paul: *You took me to my first game. You're married to my big sister; you've been faithful to her. You're the father to my first ever nephew, and two more kids since. You've driven me all over the country following Chelsea. You've sacrificed the football because you're bringing up three kids.* I point at Chris: *You're my best friend. What you have been through, I could never cope with going through. We've watched you deal with all the shit that life has thrown at you and I've been able to do nothing about it – I haven't been able to take away the pain and I've seen you broken and I've been helpless.* I've welled up, and I don't care. *I had a feeling this would happen, and it has. I've already made my decision because I cannot physically go. I need one of you with me tonight in case I have a wobble* (I take the ticket out my pocket) *while the other one gets to goes to the match. You decide.* Their mouths fall open. I copy what Fingers said, grinning: *It's not a fuckin' photocopy.* George starts saying to me: *You go, you go.* I tell him it's non-negotiable. They both want to know how I got the ticket; I relay Fingers' story. George says we should draw lots to see who should go, they both convince me that I need to draw, too. I concede to compromise, but I know it will be one of those two that will go. Tall Paul quotes from Acts chapter 1 in the Bible: *So, to replace Judas Iscariot, they nominated two men – Justus and Matthias. Then they prayed – LORD YOU KNOW EVERYONE'S HEART, SHOW US WHICH OF THESE TWO YOU HAVE CHOSEN – then they cast lots, and the lot fell to Matthias.*

We all burst out laughing. George pats his pockets and looks around for inspiration. On the table nestling beside him is a lump of celery. It's not just any lump of celery. Again, I shake my head in disbelief because hundreds of pieces are strewn both inside across the pub floor and outside here in the beer garden. Browning, dirty, stepped on, old pieces of celery. Yet, here, on the table, was a huge green lump as if it had been placed just for this moment. It was extraordinary. George picks it up, holds it out and declares:

LET THE CELERY DECIDE.

With his giant hand, he splits the celery into three pieces, turns his back to us to mix them up, faces us again with the sticks clutched in his big, hairy claws. He holds his arms out – the arms that supported hands that held the short straw for a ticket to the match. Two long lumps of celery, one short. I drew first – a long piece. *Told you* I said. *One of you two goes.* Paul draws. A long piece. George is left with the small piece, and the match-ticket. We all embrace laughing into each other's sweat. *BOUNCE IN A MINUTE! WE'RE GONNA BOUNCE IN A MINUTE!* All the Chelsea in the beer garden join in, unaware of the momentous experience we've just been through. When the bouncing subsides, George goes inside the bar to find Fingers and buy as many people as he can a drink. Not long after, those with tickets start to make a move. Tall Paul and I say bye to George, Mascot Tommy, Taxi Alan and Vastly Intelligent Keef. Lurking in the back of all of our minds are positive thoughts for the ill kid and his worried Dad by now in a Munich hospital. In some ways it didn't feel right to celebrate getting a ticket. Paul and I head back towards Odeonsplatz – Chelsea blue is absolutely everywhere in the streets. We turn towards the infamous Feldherrnhalle statues draped in Chelsea flags with hundreds gathered pre-match, singing and drinking as if it was the last game on Earth and everything had to be savoured accordingly. Two lads have climbed on the back of both of the lions, drinks in hand and singing with gusto, a line of eight POLIZIE in green uniforms under black vests (holding handcuffs and pepper spray) are taking more than a little interest. A memorable *One Man Went to Mow* belts out, everyone crouched down as they sing – the noise reverberating under the roof of the Feldherrnhalle – *Chelsea! Chelsea! Chelsea!* One of the lads on the back of a lion is clad in a purple polo; blue and white chequered flag in one hand, bottle of German lager in the other – *Chelsea!*

Chelsea! Chelsea! I kind of wish that I was up there with him. (In the days and weeks that followed, I'd marvel at the photographs taken later in the day in and around Odeonsplatz. Sitting in my kitchen on my laptop, I read about the history of the area, the Feldherrnhalle monument and so forth. I watched a haunting video from 1937 of Hitler laying a wreath, thousands of soldiers lined up in the square, fresh SS recruits taking their oath of loyalty to Adolf in front of the memorial.)

Tall Paul nods towards a shop and we go in for food and drink and head towards a park. A mass of Chelsea in the street, at least a thousand, are singing and kicking a football high in the air. The Old Bill are trying to confiscate it, one officer runs to collect it, a fan gets there first and launches it high into the Munich sky to huge cheers. Childishly hilarious. We walk further on, a cameraman moves in front of a group of lads singing, he's trying to capture some pre-match footage, could be SKY or BBC or ITV, I don't know. As he moves up close, he's definitely invading the space of the gathered friends – it's a stupid move on his part. Cups of lager are strewn at him all hitting the target – *OI, FUCK OFF* – he ducks but it's too late; he walks off dripping to search and try again with another group, wiping drink from his face as he goes, camera pointed to the floor. No-one wants that invasion, there's no-one in jester hats here wanting to be on the box: *MURDOCH, MURDOCH YOU'RE A CUNT* is sung with passion – tells you everything you need to know about proper supporters increasingly pissed off with SKY dictating kick-off times. Walking into the park, Paul proudly announces that 'hofgarten' means 'courtyard garden' and we head for some shade to lie in. A couple in conversation are strolling towards us – the guy is wearing the national football team of Argentina – sky blue and white stripes, the AFA badge covered in black and gold. I ask them if they speak English, they do. I make a quick win by explaining that I've worked in Buenos Aires on three occasions, each time for two weeks. I tell him he's about to walk into a thousand half-pissed Englishman, and then two thousand more around Odeonsplatz, maybe twenty thousand are spread across the City. He asks me if there will be a problem wearing his shirt. I say undoubtedly. Paul shrugs his shoulders in an apology to regretful Argentine eyes. His partner talks to him in quick Spanish. I turn as they pass; he has MESSI 10 on the back, would have been even worse if he had MARADONA printed on it, he takes off his shirt and folds it – she stuffs it in her bag. We pass a fountain and what looks like a temple, stone arches with a pale blue roof; a statue perched on the top. (I learn later it's called the Dianatempel; a twelve-sided gazebo from the Renaissance period, built in 1613-1617.) Paul and I watch couples dance the Tango, their battery powered stereo providing the music. It takes me back to Buenos Aires in an instant, I zone out and see Josie eating ice-cream from a tub with a small, green plastic spoon at two in the morning, I've got a bottle of Quilmes in my palm, we watch a Tango unfold on the humid streets, the adoring crowd enchanted; a man on a bicycle struggles past, he's towing a trailer piled high with plastic and aluminium recycling secured with taught orange rope – he'll sell it on for a few pesos to fund large jugs of local red wine – cycling to recycle. One time I was taken to Fuerte Apache – a sprawling estate where Carlos Teves was born – crooked teeth and burnt skin playing his way out of the toughest neighbourhood in the City to represent Boca Juniors. It was a no-go area for the Police. Catholic shrines decorated the streets where loved ones had been gunned down. My hosts told me not to speak and to keep my camera in my pocket – thankfully my dark hair and healthy tan meant I looked like a local rather than a tourist – but if the wrong person heard my native language the worst-case scenario was I'd be sliced up before I could say God Save the Queen.

Lying on the grass, I tell Paul I'll have a doze. I'm exhausted by the day so far, I haven't been this active in a day since Barcelona, a few weeks ago. It's a nice twenty-three degrees. I sleep without dreams, the distant sound of a Tango mix rocking me to sleep, a large steak and a bottle of red wine my last thought before Paul gently rocked my shoulder awake much later.

We walk to the tube at Odeonsplatz, now the red of ticketless Bayern fans were everywhere, crammed together and drinking, singing in English about football coming home and then about Bayern give us a goal. Nauseating. Paul explains it is only five stops to where Oktoberfest is held (nearest stop Theresienwiese) but I said there was no way I was getting on a tube; I could meet him there. He said it was okay, we'd walk together, it took us half an hour to reach our destination. The venue at Oktoberfest could hold five thousand people – it was full of Chelsea. Banners everywhere. As we walked through, I counted six fans passed out; hammered drinking all day on the strong, German beer. The ever-efficient Germans, you've got to admire them, had erected two huge screens to show the match, but only one of them was working. A fellow supporter told us there'd been a massive sing-song an hour ago, people had fallen over, and the screen had gone out. They were trying to get it fixed, the other one was working fine, though. The team news is announced. He's picked Ryan Bertrand. Unbelievable, go on, son! The fellow supporter asks me what I think, I say I'm prepared for the worst. He reminds me: *John Terry, Ivanovic, Mierles and Ramires are all suspended. It's a fucking tragedy for them. And for us.* I've tried not to think about it, but right now it hurts. He's picked David Luiz – he hasn't played since 15th April when he was stretchered off injured in the FA Cup semi against Spurs. Gary Cahill is out there, too. He hasn't played since he limped off injured on the 24th April against Barcelona. Bobby Di Matteo and Eddie Newton have patched a team together in the European Cup Final.

Petr Čech; Ashley Cole; José Bosingwa; David Luiz; Gary Cahill; Frank Lampard (Capt.); Ryan Bertrand; Jon Obi Mikel; Juan Mata; Salamon Kalou; Didier Drogba. Subs: Ross Turnbull; Paulo Ferreira; Michael Essien; Oriol Romeu; Florent Malouda; Fernando Torres; Daniel Sturridge.

Chapter Ten

THE EUROPEAN CUP FINAL

Saturday 19th May 2012

As Chelsea kickoff a shot of electricity crackles from my head to my feet as the roar of the ticketless masses before me deafens the Munich sky. We are shrouded in an extraordinary, heady mixture of adrenalin and hope – in reality (on paper) we could be in for a long and dreadful night – but, whatever the outcome this evening, we'll always have that semi-final branded in our bones. I light a cigarette holding it in my right hand, I put my orange Clipper in my pocket and tuck my left hand under my right armpit. My original Le Coq Sportif blue kit that Larry gave me over twenty years ago is stretching slightly as a quick shivery dash of nerves sizzles around my tense body. It's all Bayern in the first five minutes. Cahill flings himself in front of Schweinsteiger to divert a goal-bound shot for a corner. Kroos hits one wide. We can't string anything together. On seven minutes, Mata has a chance to clip a ball over, two men in space, not enough height on it; AGONISING! Then Gómez heads over. Čech denies Robben – the TV shows a close-up of our former winger with his fingers in his mouth, biting down on them in disbelief he didn't score. Thomas Müller exaggerates a fall, the ref awards a free kick, Luiz the culprit – it's a free kick but Müller is one huge unlikeable bundle of arrogance. The type of prick that dives over like he's ice-skating in flip flops and then waves an imaginary yellow in front of the ref to get his opponent booked. It's hard to decide between him and Franck Ribéry on which one you'd like to launch first head on into a giant wasp's nest. On the half-hour, a glimmer of hope as Bertrand steams forward, but he loses possession. It provokes Bayern to fly forward in attack. Bosingwa brilliantly blocks from Müller. A geezer next to Tall Paul tells us that Müller is a massive tosser. Then – Gary Cahill! What are you doing up there? He's scythed down! Free-kick! Chance! Mata spoons it over. The replay shows Drogba peeling off down the right, Mata could have slotted him in. There's ten minutes of the half left – we've got to get to half-time. Munich keep pushing forward, it's wave after wave of attack. Ribéry blasts one wide, the whole of the Oktoberfest crowd gives the odious cretin the wanker sign. A minute later, Müller sticks another wide. How's that not one nil to them? Now Kalou is in the box! Square it! He shoots limply on target, keeper has it covered. A few minutes later, Gómez has a great chance, he blows it. Müller wants a penalty coz Luiz has done him in the build-up. The crowd sings: *Fuck off, Müller! Fuck off Müller!* The half ends 0-0. Bayern have had sixty percent possession. Ashley Cole and Jon Obi Mikel are immense; Ryan Bertrand is holding his own; David Luiz and Gary Cahill are out on their feet; their hamstrings must be screaming. I say to Paul: *Sod this, bruv, I need a drink, I can't do this anymore.* I walk around, all the bars are shut. No-one is serving. No staff to be seen. No queues. Nothing. I looked to the heavens and laugh. The place has either been drunk dry or the POLIZIE have said no more. I return to my position standing next to Paul. We're basically right at the back, the last line, hundreds and hundreds of fans in front of us on chairs and on picnic benches and standing all around each side in a giant semi-circle. The second screen is still broken, the engineer has given up. Maybe they're not so efficient after all. Paul says he wonders how George is. We raise an invisible toast to him, Fingers, Lorch and all their crew from the Augustiner am Dom boozer, Taxi Alan and Mascot Tommy, Vastly Intelligent Keef and his best friend Champagne Les. The second half starts, more of the same, but at 0-0 anything can happen. The crowd implore once more: *Come on Chelsea! Come on Chelsea!*

Fifty seconds into the second half and Bayern are in – David Luiz with another block from shit-face (Ribéry) – wanker-chops (Müller) was free on the back post. Fifty minutes in and Drogba shoots with a hit and hope. Speculative. No recreation of those world-class goals at Goodison Park this time, but you could see that's what he was trying. Another flurry of Bayern attacks come in. Ashley Cole tackles Gómez brilliantly in the box. A minute later, Cole blocks a shot, it rebounds to dickhead (Ribéry) who scores. The flag is up! *You Thought You Had Scored! You Were Wrong, You Were Wrong!* Fifty-eight minutes and Cole AGAIN with a world-class block on Robben. Robben has got a proper taste for it – he has another shot-on target with his magic left peg; Čech saves. Minute seventy-three and Kalou fluffs a shot when he should've probably squared it to Mata. Groans fill the air. Plastic cups of lager thrown in anguish. Cries of frustration abound. Was that our chance? Malouda is on for Bertrand. Well done, kid. Anyone who is sitting down rises to applaud Ryan Bertrand and as his replacement runs on, (surely not 100% fit or he would've started), he is welcomed with his song, written by Stan and transferring successfully from the pub to the ground: *Florent Malouda ouda-ouda! Florent Malouda!* I know that Stan and all the others I greeted on the back row in the Nou Camp when we were all locked in are at the match. I imagine them singing along, too. In the next few minutes, Cole AGAIN to the rescue putting off twat-features (Müller) who then has a header saved by Čech. It's desperate. And then it happens. Müller scores and it's shambolic, but you can't really complain – *it's been coming* says a bloke in front of me who turns around to tell me something I already know. I nod and light a cigarette. Cole was drawn towards Gómez which leaves the prick at the back post to somehow make a shit header bounce up and in. *Fuck it.* I watch the replay of the goal and wince. Torres comes on for Kalou. Immediately, Arjen Robben has an opportunity to seal it, but he doesn't get hold of it; Čech smothers. Then Mikel elegantly moves forward, he finds Mata who has dropped deep to receive it, he lays it off to Torres who beats one man and then wins a corner. Mata jogs over. *Come on, Chelsea! COME ON, CHELSEA!* The ref blows his whistle before Mata can take it. Mata steps back, hands on hips. The ref has a stern word with jostling players from both teams. Finally, Mata swings it in – Drogba rises, heads it; *DROGBAAAAAAAAAA!!!! DROGBA!!!!!! YES! YEEEEEES!!!!!* The Oktoberfest garden absolutely falls, everyone caves into each other *YEEEES! YEEEEEESSSSS!!!!!* People have collapsed all over the gaff – and so too now does the TV. With an electric pop, the screen goes dead. It's all black. The fucking TV has blown. *Run! RUN!* Paul urges, instincts taking over – we sprint round the corner – both TVs are broken and the one that just went pop has undoubtedly gone to Sony heaven. I run straight into Tom Broadbent, (once of Wandsworth, now lives in the North West), who is running towards the broken screens – *SCREEN'S GONE, TOM!* I yell. *This way!* Paul shouts.

(About eight years later, I study Google maps to check how long the walk is from the Oktoberfest venue to Augustine am Dom. It says twenty-nine minutes. We jogged it in about fifteen minutes. I have no recollection of why we didn't stop at the first available bar. Maybe there weren't any. Maybe they were so rammed they weren't letting anyone else in – I can't remember. So, Paul's logic was to go back to the bar we'd spent all day in.)

Panting, we arrive back at Augustiner am Dom. North West Tom hadn't followed. The heavy, wooden door was shut. I bang on it, slapping my palm on the wood. It pulls ajar. *No entry* says the voice. *I've been in here all day; I just want a Coke.* The door slams shut with a crack. Paul bursts out laughing in disbelief. I light a cigarette in resignation. *Come on,* Paul says. We speed walk around the corner, a couple of fans are passed out on the pavement propped up against a wall. There's a few bodies standing by a window, we jog up to it, there's an open door, about a hundred people in the bar, plenty of room, I look up at the screen – there's a close-up of Drogba – the ref is brandishing him a yellow card, the camera zooms back out – they've got a penalty. *HE'S GIVEN A PEN!* I shout. *IT'S A FUCKIN' PEN,* I wail. Everyone is so battered, no-one realises. *What happened?* Me and Paul are asking in desperation; *What's going on?* Extraordinarily, no-one can tell us! *Is it still 1-1?* I plead. *Yeah, must be, fink so,* slurs a reply. You couldn't make this up. Every head watches the replay, now. Drogba has clipped that bell-end Ribéry. It's a penalty, no doubt. As Ribéry is helped off injured, the whole boozer graciously bays a *fuck off* to him. Olić comes off the bench. Oh Didier, what are you doing? Sent off in Moscow, brings down Fàbregas in the Nou for Messi's pen, and now this. I can see no other outcome than a goal – but it's early enough in extra-time to pull it back again, Drogba and Torres up front, Malouda with fresh legs. Jon Obi is holding the ball, he won't hand it to Robben, he's remonstrating with him, saying something, and then the camera pans away. Eventually, Robben places the ball – a wonderful player for us back in the day. The whole pub has sobered up in about twenty seconds. A huge hush descends. I put my hands behind my head. Robben runs up. He blasts it – Petr saves! THE BALL'S LOOSE! ČECH FALLS ON THE BALL!!!! *HE'S SAVED IT! HE'S SAVED IT!* Shit, I can't cope – I've just run here and now this happens. Me and Paul are jumping up and down, there's people piling into us, he's fucking saved it, the place has gone berserk. I watch the replay, there's a yellow inflatable ball thrown from our end just as Robben runs up – my mind races to how George must be feeling – what about the thousands of people at the Oktoberfest venue – they probably don't even know it's happened. The first half of extra time finishes. Everyone is dead on their feet – and I'm talking about all of us in the boozer. What a find this place is. *Thank you, Jesus.* Paul buys a beer – he still offers me one out of habit – I'm all right. I go out for a quick cigarette. There's an Irish guy in his twenties totally off his face, slurring and unsteady – I get him up to speed on proceedings and grab him a large water from the bar. Second half of extra-time begins. Drobga is down injured on the far side but the krauts aren't going to kick this one out. Instead, Lahm clips it over to Olić in the box. Time stands still. He plays it across the six-yard box but there's too much on it. If he pulls it back – they're in. We've massively got away with one there. I say to Paul: *Luiz and Cahill are done.* As soon as I say that, Cahill absolutely flings himself across Gómez and it bounces off him to Luiz who boots it clear for a corner. The minutes tick by. And it's penalties.

I go to the bar and place my hands on the top, I take a deep breath and hold it down in my lungs for *two, three, four* and then I exhale *two, three, four, five, six*. The barman raises an eyebrow. I order two double whisky's – *Scottish single malt please, not that JD piss*. The barman smiles at me. I tell him I haven't had a drink since March. I don't care if he believes me or not but he wishes Chelsea good luck. I hand one of the glasses to Paul, the aroma rising to my nose, a scent of wood and sherry. He refuses it; says he can't drink it. This has never happened in the history of our relationship. A guy appears in front of me, animated as anything, probably been on the packet, his blonde hair is clipped short, he's a little sunburnt, he's gibbering excitedly in front of me, he reminds me of a Swedish lad the Doris and I met when travelling Australia in 2005, we were both well fond of him, I smile as he keeps repeating: *Will Torres take a PK?* I'm like: *Eh?* And he's saying: *Will Torres take a PK?* I say: *Mate, I've got no idea.* (It isn't until it's all over that I realise that by PK he meant Penalty Kick.) I stand with a double Scotch in each hand. Lahm, their Captain, walks up; places the ball with a spin; makes sure he's happy. He treads backwards a few paces; stops; hands on hips; spits on the pitch; rubs his nose, runs up.... Ooooo, Čech is so, so close to it, but it's 1-0 to Bayern. I drink whisky. Then more. It burns my throat. It hits my stomach. Mata looks nervous. I neck the rest of the whisky from the first glass, move over and place the empty vessel on the bar. I return to Paul's side. I lean in: *He missed his last pen, didn't he?* And Paul nods as I say pessimistically: *Left foot* and Paul says: *Pearce and Waddle in Italia '90*. We're both thinking the same. Neuer is jumping under his crossbar, he looks as relaxed as they come, his long arms high in the air psyching out our Juan. The keeper saves. The wall of red behind Neuer's goal goes mental. They know. We know. We're fucked. By the time Gómez has put the ball on the spot, I've necked the second whisky. My stomach lurches a little. I close my eyes, embracing the warm fuzz in my head. I open my eyes. Čech goes the right way but it's a perfect penalty. We're two nil down and it's a long way home. I put the second empty glass on the bar and then I turn with my back to the wall, ignoring the TV. *Who's next?* I say to Paul. *Luiz* is walking up, he replies. *My favourite player*, I reply. I breathe, turn back around, Luiz has got the longest run up planned I've ever seen. *This is going over....* says half the pub at the same time – the Swedish lad bursts out laughing at this, and then says to me with glazed blue eyes: *To be fair, if he doesn't score, you're fucked.* Someone shouts in wild frustration, voice cracked, throat hoarse, nerves shot to pieces: *Fucks sake, Chelsea. Lampard should be taking this!* He's got a point. I force myself to look. Neuer still looks massive in that goal. Here we go. Wallop! What a fucking penalty! The Swedish lad grabs my shoulders in delight – *I hate these fucking Germans* he tells me. The relief in the pub is palpable, like the air escaping an airbed when you're a kid and you've pulled the plug and belly flopped on it; but then almost instantly everyone fears that it's probably just delayed the inevitable. The tangible swing in emotion is incredible. From renewed hope (when Luiz absolutely smashed the penalty home) to processing the reality of the situation (the krauts not missing any of their pens, their keeper saving another one of ours) we are now back to the fear and the reality of losing. Paul nods to the TV – *their keeper is taking it.* Neuer verses Čech. I've got a good feeling about this one. Hope tentatively rises again in the pub. People start bouncing on their toes: *COME ON PETR!* I look to my right, a bloke has his palms together as if in prayer, finger tips resting on his chin and he's repeating in a whisper: *Please, please, please, please, please....* Čech goes the right way AGAIN and for a split-second it looks like he's got it covered! Some cheer thinking he's saved it, but the ball nestles in the net; the red wall celebrates; the German keeper soaks in the adoration; swear he tries to stare out Čech as he walks back to face the next Chelsea penalty. I turn my back to the wall and the screen again. Paul says: *Frank Lampard* and I think that's good because we need this one to stay in with a chance and he's our best penalty taker. I turn and watch. I notice for the first time two fellas under the screen looking at us to see our reaction. They can't watch the TV so they are watching us. Super Frank smashes it home. The pub releases a *YES,* hands are clapped together thick and fast and then eerie silence descends briefly for a while like a blanket over a child to soothe them; then the deft sound of trainers padding on wooden flooring is evident as people nervously shift the weight from one foot on to the other. Here comes the sub, Olić – number eleven, hands on hips – *left foot*, I say, and as if someone has flicked a switch people start to wrap their arms around each other like the Chelsea players in the centre-circle and the rest of the squad and staff on the touchline. Someone at the rear of the pub starts screaming: *COME ON! COME ON!* I look to my right and the bloke is still in prayer whispering: *Please, please, please, please, please....* I happen to look again beneath the TV screen, the two fellas are still standing under it – they continue to face opposite us but now they've got their heads down – it's not just the screen that they can't look at, they can't look at us now, either, so they look to the floor. It suddenly goes quiet as Olić pushes off for his run up; *Please, please, please, please, please....* ČECH SAVES IT! *HE'S SAVED IT!!!* He's clawed the bastard away! The fellas under the TV screen are embracing in a hug and then assume their position facing all of us. I turn again to Paul. I don't have to ask who is next, he states calmly: *Ashley Cole* and I say: *Eh? Not Torres?* Paul shakes his head and then the emotion bubbles up, he screams: *Come on Ashley!* And it catches around the pub: *Come on, Ashley! COME ON, ASHLEY!* I happen to look to my left out of the window – a threatening line of POLIZEI in their green uniforms with black riot padding over the top stand motionless and stare menacingly – I snap my head back to the box and say in deflated desperation: *Left foot* and this causes me to look to the floor, head facing down. I put my forehead on Paul's chest and he says: *Watch it! Watch it!* I turn around in resignation, Neuer still looks like a giant in the goal mouth, I hear the whispering monk repeating: *Please, please, please, please, please....* Cole stutters and *SCORES! HE SCORES!!!!* It's three-three! The Swedish fella dances in front of me: *Fucking hell, my friend! It is three-three.* The Chelsea patrons in this humble establishment resume position with arms around each other; defiant cries of hope for our keeper Petr Čech fill the air. Sure enough, the two fellas under the TV screen aren't looking at the screen, but they're not looking at the floor either – the have geed each other up and they are facing us. We'll deliver the message. I nod at them and grimace, shake a fist of hope and courage. The camera pans in on Schweinsteiger. I break the silence: *Look at his face! He's missing this.... he's missing this......* He stutters his run-up before striking it.... *IT'S OFF THE POST! YEEEES!* There is celebration amongst us, but it's not like the pandemonium that ensued in here when Čech saved Robben's penalty in extra-time. Everyone remembers Moscow. For that penalty shoot-out, Tall Paul and I stood next to each other, too. The TV shows a replay of Schweinsteiger's effort – Čech got a touch, he actually saved it. What a hero. Here we are again. I turn to Paul and look at the floor. *Drogba*, he says. I turn and look at the TV. The two fellas under the screen are now arm-in-arm, looking at the floor and kicking their feet out as if shaking the nerves out of their toes. Paul and I put our arms around each other. If he misses, it's sudden-death. Again. I can't see or hear the whispering monk. I feel my throat tightening, I stand on tip-toes, the nervous energy filling the air from everyone in here is a defining spiritual moment for everyone. Didier Drogba. Sent off in Moscow. Equalised tonight. Gave away a pen in the semi *and* in the final. Camera shows a close-up. He pulls his socks up. He looks confident. Camera switches to the bigger picture. Hands on hips. Not much of a run-up. I smile thinking of Luiz's barmy sprint and shot in the top corner. In the split-second silence here in the pub, we hear the shrill blast of referee's whistle as he blows. *COME ON, DIDIER*....

YEEEEEEEEEEEEEEEEEEESSSSSSSSSSSSSS!!!!!!!

Arms, limbs and bodies collide – the breath sucked out of everyone until the lungs can roar again in celebration. I open my eyes and I realise I'm still hugging Tall Paul and we have somehow travelled over to the side of the bar by the toilets by a huge mirror, a mass of movement all around, I'm staring at the reflection of myself and I realise I'm crying. I'm not the only one. The whispering monk is shedding jubilant tears. We swing round towards the exit still jumping and shouting in celebration, a bloke has stripped naked, running around in circles outside, the POLIZEI have dispersed, nowhere to be seen, they know and I know the pub might have been smashed up if Bayern had won, there are fans on their knees, there are fans in disbelief, there is a bloke running around naked. There is no sense of time. There is no sense of reality. It's like I'm stewing in one of my dreams. Suddenly Tall Paul is pulling my shirt and speaking into my ear, dragging me away: *Shit! We've got to go; we've got to go.*

We are on a train, I have got no idea how I got on it, but I'm sitting next to Paul who keeps checking his watch, we've got to get to Fröttmaning before the coach departs, we had one hour from the final whistle. *We did it, we won it*, Paul laughs. And then with a guffaw, I almost choke on my laughter because I've remembered something and Paul asks me what and I say: *Spurs drop into the Europa* and he cracks up: *ARE YOU WATCHING, ARE YOU WATCHING, ARE YOU WATCHING WHITE HART LANE?* At a station, the door opens and a family get on, they sit adjacent to us, the Dad eyes us nervously – his kid is wrapped in a huge Bayern scarf – he looks miserable and tired, wet cheeks glisten from the tears he's shed, the worried wife is speaking in hushed, Bavarian tones. I stand up and sit opposite Paul so I'm facing the kid – I wink at the parents, giving them a reassuring smile, saying: *It's all right.* I say *Hey* to him, he looks at me, must be about eight or nine years old, I tell him that four years ago Chelsea lost in a penalty shoot-out to Manchester United – his eyes widen – he says: *Really?* I tell him that Bayern are a really good team – and I hand him a two Euro coin that I'd fished out my pocket and held in my palm. He takes it and smiles and says thanks. *Danke.* I tell him it's okay to be upset, Bayern will probably win it next season. He says: *Do you think so?* And I say. *Yes, I think so.* Paul says we have to change train at Münchner Freiheit station. I nod at the parents and the Dad extends his hand, we shake and then he shakes hands with Paul. I look at the Mum who sweeps her hair behind her ear and looks at me with bright eyes – the fear has gone from her face to be replaced with gratitude. She says: *Have a safe journey home* as we step off to change trains.

When we get to the coach park, George is waiting for us outside the coach. We all embrace. *We did it! We did it! We did it!* Huddled now, Paul is grinning, something has crossed his mind, and George says: *What?* Paul starts to walk up the steps into the coach and replies: *It would be a great title for a book* and George and I say: *What would?* And Tall Paul turns around dramatically on the coach steps before going to find his seat and replies: *LET THE CELERY DECIDE.*

EPILOGUE

George tells his side of the story

FIFTY-THREE HOURS – LET THE CELERY DECIDE

I was working in Epsom, Surrey as a teacher – and back on April 24th 2012 I was in charge of a Sixth Form Geography Field Trip to Swanage, Dorset. Bizarrely enough, I found myself in a room with a dozen 17-year-olds listening to Radio 5 live when Gary Neville *"ooooooohhhhed"* and 'scoregasmed' his way to announcing Torres's goal away at Barcelona which sent Chelsea through to their second Champions League Final. We'd finished the night's teaching early, (on the subject of 'Old Harry Rocks' on the Isle of Purbeck in Dorset), to allow the substantial teenage Chelsea cohort to listen to the match on the radio. I am CRB (now DBS) checked, but I must confess that for a couple of minutes I was embracing the Chelsea supporting students as if I were at The Bridge. The wait for the final whistle was brilliant.

My two long-time Chelsea travel buddies Larry and Walter were out there, (as you've read), and once Larry's videos began to be posted on Facebook it brought it home to me what this meant. We were to compete in another Champions League final, it was so painful last time. Not a chance of winning the Cup this time though, not against Bayern in their own backyard. I never really thought about going. Not sure why. I've never really been able to go to European away games due to being a teacher. I've often thought about a cheeky bunk but I know that the TV cameras would find me and I'd have a lot of explaining to do on a Thursday morning! I love being a teacher and have never yet been to a game where I haven't bumped into a student that I teach, or used to teach, singing: *"Sir, give us a song! Sir, Sir, give us a song!"*

It was Walts that texted me first: "Mate, we can get a coach with from London to Munich for £129 return. Let's go and watch it in Munich!" It quickly dawned on me that as the final was on a Saturday night, this might be the opportunity I'd never had. I created a lengthy jobs list:

1 – Chat with wife. (She'd be fine.)

Easy. Walts texted back: "The coaches leave at 3:00pm on the Friday. Can you get time off work?" Oh, shit. No way. You can't just take time off as a teacher. I'd have to leave at 1:00pm to be sure. I had a lesson at 2:00pm. Could another member of staff cover me? Should I ask my Head teacher? He's a Fulham fan, he is pretty reasonable – so, I asked him. He put the ball back in my court and asked me to see if there was another way. (So, it wasn't a 'no' from him.) I texted Walts back. It looked OK. Tall Paul had got clearance from Bomber command. Larry was surprisingly quiet. Walts texted me again – the coaches stopped at Maidstone Services at 4:30pm. Boom. I could leave school at 3.00pm and make it. I texted my Head to let him know that I didn't need time off. Should I park in Maidstone? The missus agreed to pick me up from my school in Epsom and take me to Maidstone. What a ledge. Trip on. There's nothing we could do to persuade Larry, something he regrets to this day.

School on Friday was a nightmare, every lesson I taught was a drag; the clock moved agonisingly slowly. At 3:00pm, the wife duly arrived and by 4:00pm we were at Maidstone services. We said our goodbyes and I called to check I hadn't missed the coach fleet – no worries, they were still on the M25. Whilst waiting outside, a bus carrying a squad of Gurkhas pulled up and they filed through. The waiting Chelsea fans (plenty of others had also booked with Coach Innovations to get picked up at Maidstone) broke into spontaneous applause, it was actually quite an emotional moment. The guy next to me who I had been chatting with let me know that: *"I'm a right fucking racist, but I love them Gurkhas!"* Coach Innovations pulled up – or as we got to call them 'Dave's Coaches' (from the comedy show 'Gavin & Stacey') – bet the Welsh drivers haven't heard that gag before! One of the drivers always pronounced our destination as "Moonik" which we adopted when singing, *"I like to Moonik Moonik!"* There was a young lad called Connor who worked on our bus bringing us beers for a pound in his polystyrene cup. He must have made loads of money!

We caught the ferry at 6:30pm – I'd imagined that this would have been a highlight of the trip but it was a little underwhelming, the highlight probably being meeting some French students and trying out my French, which they didn't understand, much to the enjoyment of the others. We arrived in Calais at 8.00pm and the next twelve hours were a haze of service stations, strip washes, beer, singing and snoozing. At 8.00am, we arrived at the Allianz Arena and had a quick wander round before picking up some Currywurst. It was then that we had the discussion. *"What happens if one of us gets a ticket and the others don't? If someone gets lucky, then good on them. Agreed? Agreed!"*

We got the tube into town, it was hot hot hot, the square was hectic, loads of Munich fans, lots of singing, it was a bit overwhelming – who should we meet up with? Where can we watch the game? When will the Munich fans just do one? We found a bar with space and a beer garden – not a clue what it was called but seemed to fit the ticket. A Lederhosen clad buxom Fräulein with perfect pig-tails was carrying half a dozen steins of beer outside – it comes in two-pint glasses! Yes! Five Euros each, don't mind if I do! We started drinking. A bunch of 50-year-olds were doing cocaine off a table, some long-haired Bayern fan came outside – the fans inside singing, *'There's only one Jack Sparrow"* at him. Outside, it continued: *"One Bon Jovi, there's only one Bon Jovi!"* and *"Oh we're half way there, oh oh livin' on a prayer!"* And, *"Whoa, shake it up, just like Bad Medicine!"* He left. I went inside to the toilet and ended up sitting on a table with a bunch of young 20-year-olds. A young man who looked like Harry Potter walked past our table with his girlfriend – cue Hermione themed songs querying how well they knew each other and what spells were shared. That sort of thing is dying with laughter funny – when you're there. Ended up that we'd met a couple of the lads before and so we shared some stories. (These lads are still the ones I love to see on the rarer forays to Chelsea these days).

At 4:00pm Walts appears and give us a big speech and then he lets us know that he had just been given a ticket to the final. WHAT? He had the Willy Wonka Golden ticket version 2.0. Sadly, a kid had been taken ill and his Dad had to take him to hospital – I had no idea how the rest of this story went until now! He gave his two tickets to Fingers Tom, one of the lads we had been Harry Pottering with, Tom then gave the second one to Walter and he was off to the Final, except that he wasn't. It couldn't have happened to a better bloke (if you know him, you know him). As you've read, he wanted either his brother-in-law, Tall Paul, to go or his old mate George. We were gobsmacked, I suggested we drew straws for it – let destiny decide. Actually, as you've read, there was some celery; we let the celery decide – this seemed by far the right thing to do.

I ended up with ticket, and that was that, I was off. But what's the time? Where do I go? How do I get there? Oh no, I'm a wee bit pissed. It was 6:00pm. I said my goodbyes, got on the tube to the stadium. The tube was hot, hot, hot. I was the only Chelsea fan on there and got ripped a new one by the Bayern fans! Some version of: *"You What? You What? You What, You What, You What?"* every time I sang (on my own). I arrived at the Olympic Stadium with the Munich fans at 6:45pm in plenty of time…. Wait, this isn't the stadium! Oh bugger, I had followed the crowd to the wrong ground (Bayern Munich's old ground) which was showing a beam back of the game. *No no no, this can't be happening!* I travelled back to the City centre to try again and this time, old muggins here arrived at the Allianz. I was drinking water to sober up as I wanted to fully enjoy the experience. On the way to the ground I got offered £1,300 for the ticket. No chance.

I saw a kid I taught, standard. Happens every time! The game was a blur but we were getting tonked. The atmosphere was amazing, Munich fans outnumbered us not surprisingly, their choreographed singing was loud but annoying and the trophy was going to them. After all, it was their ground, their trophy and that obnoxious banner let us know. Anyway, we'd had a lot of suspensions and injuries so our team was nowhere near what it had been. Great day out though. After all, *'Ryan like a Lion in Bayern'* was playing. Some lady behind me was moody and spent the whole game sat down and, get this, on her mobile phone! This made me mad. And then Drogba scored. What. The. Actual. As extra-time started, nerves that had just been marinating deep in my psyche began to be unbearable. And then Petr saved Robben's penalty. What. The. Actual. Hang on, now extra-time is over and it's gone to penalties; we can win this on pens, can't we?

I was sat next to a Dad with his son who was (also) called Chris. Little Chris had Downs Syndrome and was nervous about how high up we were in the stand; so, he felt like he was hanging on for dear life – he was proper Chels. After the first few pens, (I was most nervous about Ashley Cole!), I found myself holding hands with Little Chris as Drogba walked up to take the last one. It was not until those few seconds that I realised that this was it. It's funny, I was so involved in the emotion, that I had lost track of what was going on.

Drogs walks up.

Bang. What? Bang. What? It's in. What? Why is Frank running towards us and not the others? What? Why is the man behind me taking all his clothes off? We've won? What? We've won? Shut up. And then the wave came. We've won, we've won. I hugged Little Chris, his Dad was crying, I hugged his Dad, I was crying, we've won the European Cup. What? Spurs are knocked out of the Champions League as well for next year? Brilliant! Where's those Munich fans now? Your yard, your trophy. *Chelsea. Chelsea. Chelsea.* How are Walter and Tall Paul? How's my son back home? Is he up? Does he understand aged 6-years-old? Have I marked those books for Monday? Celebrations, JT full kit, Bobby de Matteo, Luiz on the bar in a stupid hat, let them lift the cup, get out of the way. Where is the coach parked? What time does it go?

I can't really remember the rest but suffice to say I made it to the coach and embraced the others. My phone had run out – later I heard the voice message from my son. We travelled home. Wow. I arrived at Clapham Junction at 6.00pm to find it filled with Chelsea fans young and old. Ha ha, of course, they had a victory parade whilst we were still travelling home. Bizarre. Got home for 8.00pm, I was back in school on Monday morning. *"How was your weekend, Sir?"* Yes fine, I believe is the correct British answer. I watched JT lift the European Cup, lads. To this day, words can't express my thanks to Walter and Fingers Tom.

I would still put the birthing of each of my children above my Munich experience but even then, not far above and that is it. I've waited eight years to write this. It's as clear today as it was then. Fifty-three hours of my life well spent if you ask me.

George aka Big Chris
August 2020

ACKNOWLEDGEMENTS

In no particular order:

Jesus; Mark Worrall GATE17; Tom Roberts; Simon Lorch; Aunty Jean Attwood; Jonathan Thatcher; Paul Barnard; Naomi Barnard (editor); Tom Morton at tommortondesign.com; Clare Smith; Les Allen; Keith Smith; Thomas Smith; Alan Thompson RIP; Richard Knowles; Doctor Wayne Morgan; Ray Burns; Edward Sokolowski; BongoJo; The Welsh lads from Coach Innovations; David Chidgey @ChelseaFanCast; David Johnstone; James Wheatley; Jeffrey Bell; Charlie Wright; Daniel Smale; Geoff Donohue; Kraig Dixon; ZOOM2020 – Paulo Sanderson MBE; Neil Beckett; Simon Gale; Gareth Hawkes; Christopher Smitheram; Andrew Smith; The Arun Church soldiers who look out for me and my family; All the Papworths and their Partners; Yates (Mum, Dad, Chloe) mob; Rebecca Joanne; Red May; Sol Benjamin.

The lyrics to the song *LEAN BACK* reproduced by kind permission from Bethel Music. All lyrics are the property and copyright of their owners. All lyrics provided for educational purposes only. Special thanks to Dion Davis. I messaged Dion via Instagram explaining I had heard him singing *Lean Back* when my YouTube (on auto-play) selected the song. Transfixed, I kept the song on repeat, wrote the busker scene in Chapter Seven, which led to the concert scene in Chapter Eight.

You can listen to the song for yourself here:
https://www.youtube.com/watch?v=YT9Gz6JaCPo
and
shorturl.at/pwX25

AUTHOR'S NOTE

Any inaccuracies (geographical, historical, or other) are purely my error. The majority of this story is factual; however, 8 (eight) long years have passed since I put pen to paper to describe the events, and it was with time on my hands due to Covid-19 that prompted me to crack on writing it. Some of the characters I met occurred at different stages of my life, but fitted well into the story. I purposefully wrote the text in the style it appears with a stream of consciousness, without speech marks and occasionally without punctuation. The DREAM chapters, although fiction, are still an accurate representation of vivid dreams I often had when whacked out on meds. The whole book is set in the middle of a mental health crisis. After over a year signed off sick, my meds gradually reduced (I'm still on a low dose) and I returned to work. So, if your car is broken, you take it to the mechanic. So, if your head needs fixing, there are places you can go to and specialists you can see. If anyone reading this is experiencing anxiety or depression or any other mental health issues, please consider visiting your GP, reaching out to acquaintances who can listen and support and, if you're feeling backed into a corner, please call the Samaritans. I have found that listening to meditations and mindfulness (as well as songs like *LEAN BACK*) have helped me enormously. You matter. YOU MATTER!

Live generously and keep the peace. There is always hope.

Walts
August 2020.

GATE 17
THE COMPLETE COLLECTION
(CHRISTMAS 2020)

CHELSEA
Over Land and Sea – Mark Worrall
Chelsea here, Chelsea There – Kelvin Barker, David Johnstone, Mark Worrall
Chelsea Football Fanzine – the best of cfcuk
One Man Went to Mow – Mark Worrall
Chelsea Chronicles (Five Volume Series) – Mark Worrall
Making History Not Reliving It –
Kelvin Barker, David Johnstone, Mark Worrall
Celery! Representing Chelsea in the 1980s – Kelvin Barker
Stuck On You: a year in the life of a Chelsea supporter – Walter Otton
Palpable Discord: a year of drama and dissent at Chelsea – Clayton Beerman
Rhyme and Treason – Carol Ann Wood
Eddie Mac Eddie Mac – Eddie McCreadie's Blue & White Army
The Italian Job: A Chelsea thriller starring Antonio Conte – Mark Worrall
Carefree! Chelsea Chants & Terrace Culture – Mark Worrall, Walter Otton
Diamonds, Dynamos and Devils – Tim Rolls
Arrivederci Antonio: The Italian Job (part two) – Mark Worrall
Where Were You When We Were Shocking? – Neil L. Smith
Chelsea: 100 Memorable Games – Chelsea Chadder
Bewitched, Bothered & Bewildered – Carol Ann Wood
Stamford Bridge Is Falling Down – Tim Rolls
Cult Fiction – Dean Mears
Chelsea: If Twitter Was Around When… – Chelsea Chadder
Blue Army – Vince Cooper
Liquidator 1969-70 A Chelsea Memoir – Mark Worrall
When Skies Are Grey: Super Frank, Chelsea And The Coronavirus Crisis – Mark Worrall
Tales Of The (Chelsea) Unexpected – David Johnstone & Neil L Smith
The Ultimate Chelsea Quiz Book – Chelsea Chadder
Blue Days – Chris Wright
Let The Celery Decide – Walter Otton

FICTION
Blue Murder: Chelsea Till I Die – Mark Worrall
The Wrong Outfit – Al Gregg
The Red Hand Gang – Walter Otton
Coming Clean – Christopher Morgan
This Damnation – Mark Worrall
Poppy – Walter Otton

NON FICTION
Roe2Ro – Walter Otton
Shorts – Walter Otton
England International Football Team Quiz & Trivia Book – George Cross

www.gate17.co.uk

Printed in Great Britain
by Amazon